JAMES BUCHANAN
1791 – 1868

Chronology – Documents – Bibliographical Aids

Edited by

IRVING J. SLOAN

Series Editor

HOWARD F. BREMER

Oceana Publications, Inc.
Dobbs Ferry, New York 10522
1968

Library of Congress Catalog Card Number 68-21537
Oceana Book No. 303-3

Printed in the United States of America

CONTENTS

EDITOR'S FOREWORD

Every attempt has been made to cite the most accurate dates in this Chronology. Diaries, documents, and similar evidence have been used to determine the exact date. If, however, later scholarship has found such dates to be obviously erroneous, the more plausible date has been used. Should this Chronology be in conflict with other authorities, the student is urged to go back to original sources as well as to such careful biographers as Philip S. Klein.

This is a research tool compiled primarily for the student. While it does make some judgments on the significance of the events, it is hoped that they are reasoned judgments based on a long acquaintance with American History.

Obviously, the very selection of events by any writer is itself a judgment.

The essence of these little books is in their making available some pertinent facts and key documents **plus** a critical bibliography which should direct the student to investigate for himself additional and/or contradictory material. The works cited may not always be available in small libraries, but neither are they usually the old, out of print, type of books often included in similar accounts. Documents in this volume are taken from: William MacDonald, *Select Documents of the History of the United States, 1776-1861,* and James D. Richardson, ed., *Messages and Papers of the Presidents. Vol. 5: Washington.* 1897.

CHRONOLOGY

1791

April 23   Born, Cove Gap in Lancaster County, Pennsylvania. Father: James Buchanan. Mother: Elizabeth Speer Buchanan.

1794

Family, now consisting of five girls in addition to young James, moved to the center of Mercersburg. Eventually, there were eleven children in the family.

1795—1805

Attended Old Stone Academy at Mercersburg where he studied under three tutors over the years.

1807

September   Entered Dickinson College in Carlisle, Pennsylvania. While in the following year he was expelled for disorderly conduct, he was shortly reinstated and thereafter his social and academic record was outstanding.

1809

September 9   Graduated from Dickinson College with Honors.

December   Arrived in Lancaster to study law with James Hopkins, leader of the Lancaster bar and noted attorney throughout the state.

1812

At the end of his apprenticeship he decided to go to Kentucky to handle a case involving his father's property in Elizabethtown.

November 17   Returned from Kentucky and was admitted to the Pennsylvania Bar to practice law.

1813

February 20   Opened his law office in Lancaster.

1

1814

August 24   Nominated by the Lancaster Federalist Party for office of State Assemblyman.

August 25   Registered as a volunteer in the War of 1812, and served in the military service for a brief period until after a battle at Baltimore.

October   Elected to the House of Representatives in Pennsylvania legislature, leading the ticket. Arrived in Harrisburg to begin his term.

1815

February 1 Delivered his first formal speech as a public official. It was so much in opposition to Federalist doctrine that he was advised to join the Democrats, which he declined to do at that time.

1816

October   Re-elected as State Assemblyman, served on the Judiciary Committee and the Committee on Banks.

1817

Returned to the practice of law and built an extensive practice over the next two years which by 1819 gave him a widely-known legal reputation.

1819

July   Became engaged to Ann Coleman, daughter of Robert Coleman, one of the country's first millionaires.

November 23 Served on local Federalist Party committee to prepare official resolutions instructing District Congressman to oppose extension of slavery to Missouri.

December   Ann Coleman broke her engagement to Buchanan in a moment of jealousy and, probably, misunderstanding.

December 9 Ann died, perhaps as the result of an overdose of drugs. Buchanan was the only President to remain a bachelor throughout his life.

1820

August 25 Nominated by the Lancaster "Republican Federalists" for the United States House of Representatives.

October Elected to Congress from district composed of Lancaster, Dauphin, and Lebanon in Pennsylvania.

1821

June 11 His father died.

December 5 Seated in the House of Representatives. Appointed to the Committee on Agriculture.

December Requested by political leaders to deliver an important speech on the Deficiency Bill in support of the policies of John C. Calhoun.

1822

January 24 Appointed Chairman of a committee of five to inquire and report concerning the collection of fines imposed by United States courts martial on militiamen in Pennsylvania for delinquincies during War of 1812.

February 14 Appointed a member of committee to investigate the Post Office Department.

March 12 Voted against amendment to the Bankruptcy Bill, admitting others than merchants to the benefits of the law. He delivered an important speech on the bill.

1823

February 28 Voted for resolution requesting the President to negotiate with the Maritime powers for the abolition of the slave trade.

December 2 Appointed member of Committee on Judiciary.

December 15 Appointed member of Select Committee of seven for the purpose of inquiring into the expediency of recommending to the States the propriety of an amendment to the Constitution making the mode of electing members of the House and Electors uniform throughout the United States.

1824

January 15 Introduced and spoke upon a Resolution for the appointment of a Committee to inquire in what way the resolutions of Congress for the erection of a monument to Washington may be best accomplished.

April 16 Voted in favor of Tariff Bill of 1824, the protective features of which evoked from Henry Clay the famous "American system" phrase.

November Re-elected for a third successive term as *Federal-Republican*. Buchanan played role as "fixer" in the presidential election which took place in the House of Representatives as a result of a lack of a majority of electoral votes for Jackson, Adams, Crawford or Clay. While he supported Jackson, Adams was elected.

1826

January 19 Voted against an amendment to the Judiciary System Bill which would have decreased the number of associate judges.

December Began his fight to organize a new Democratic party in Pennsylvania, amalgamating the Federalist German farmers of the East and the Scotch-Irish frontier Democrats of the Western part of the state.

1828

February 4 Opened his fifth campaign for Congress with a speech in Congress attacking President Adams, which made him known throughout the country as a powerful champion of Jackson.

May 27 Federalists and Republicans in Lancaster united as a single Democratic Party, and Buchanan ran for office for the first time as a Democrat.

October Re-elected Congressman by overwhelming majority in the district as a Democrat after being elected four times as a Federalist. Andrew Jackson's winning of Pennsylvania in the presidential election was attributed to Buchanan.

1830

January 14   Prepared a Minority Report opposing a proposal by his own House Judiciary Committee which would have abrogated Section 25 of the Judiciary Act of 1789 and thereby limited the national jurisdiction of the Supreme Court. His Report continuing national jurisdiction was adopted by the full House, 138-51.

1831

June 12   Accepted an appointment from President Andrew Jackson to serve as Minister to Russia. He spent much of the year learning French and studying trade problems with Russia.

1832

January 12   Nomination to the Russian Mission was confirmed by the United States Senate.

June 2   Arrived in St. Petersburg after several weeks of touring England.

December 18   Concluded a Commercial Treaty with Russia, the first agreement of its kind which the Russian Imperial Government had made with any nation.

1833

May 14   His mother died.

August 5   Had his last audience with Emperor Nicholas, concluding mission to Russia.

August 8   Left St. Petersburg and spent time touring Paris and London en route to the United States.

November 24   His ship, the *Susquehanna,* docked in Philadelphia. Buchanan honored that same evening with a $5-a-plate homecoming dinner.

December 7   Defeated in the Pennsylvania State legislature election for United States Senator.

1834

December 15   Appeared as a Senator from Pennsylvania to fill a vacancy, qualified, and took his seat.

1835

Spent a good deal of time and energy through the year rebuilding his political power in Pennsylvania.

December 17   Became member of the Judiciary Committee in the Senate.

1836

March 11   Made motion in the Senate which resulted in defeat of Calhoun's "gag rule" directed against abolitionist petitions.

November   Martin Van Buren elected President on the Democratic ticket.

December   Buchanan became the first person to receive second election from legislature of Pennsylvania, returning for a second term in the United States Senate.

December 14   Made a member of the Committee on the District of Columbia.

1837

Chosen Chairman of the Senate Foreign Relations Committee.

December 29   Delivered speech in the Senate favoring the admission of Michigan into the Union.

1838

January 29   Presented a petition for the abolition of slavery in the District of Columbia.

April 23   Made a speech on power of the Bank of the United States under its Pennsylvania charter in support of the bill to prevent it from re-issuing and circulating the notes of the old bank.

November   Most of the month spent attending to family problems, as he had taken on the major responsibility for caring for a number of young nephews and nieces as the result of deaths among his brothers and sisters.

December   Refused Van Buren's offer to appoint him Attorney General.

1840

November — William Henry Harrison elected President on the Whig ticket, defeating Van Buren, thus deflating Buchanan's aspirations for the Democratic nomination that year.

1841

April 4 — John Tyler succeeded to the presidency upon the death of Harrison one month after the latter was inaugurated. Buchanan began to look toward the presidential nomination in the next election in 1844, and much of his activity from time forward was aimed at that goal.

December 29 — Delivered speech in the Senate against the establishment of "exchequer board" proposal by the Secretary of the Treasury.

1842

August 20 — Voted against ratificiation of the Webster-Ashburton Treaty on the ground that American rights had been compromised.

December 5 — Re-elected to the United States Senate.

1844

May 28 — James K. Polk received the Democratic Party nomination for president. Buchanan did not actively compete, but offered his name if Van Buren withdrew from the battle. The latter could not obtain enough votes and the convention compromised on Polk.

November — Polk elected. Buchanan campaigned hard for him to assure his own influence in the next administration.

1845

February 17 — Received letter from President Polk inviting him to accept appointment of Secretary of State.

Delivered his last speech in the Senate in favor of the resolutions for the immediate annexation of Texas.

March 6 — Senate confirmed his appointment as Secretary of State.

September — Requested Polk to appoint him to fill a vacancy on the United States Supreme Court. Later, in November, withdrew request.

November 7   Recommended Slidell Mission to Mexico for the secret purpose of purchasing Upper California and New Mexico as well as to adjust United States boundary with Mexico along the Rio Grande in Texas.

1846

January 23   Held a grand ball marking the major social event of the year in Washington.

February 26   Announced that the United States was ready to reopen discussion with Great Britain on the Oregon boundary if she would take the initiative.

June 10   Polk lay the British proposal for a settlement of the Oregon question before the Senate. This was Buchanan's recommendation supported by the Cabinet.

June 15   Senate ratified Oregon Treaty.

June 28   He again asked for a Supreme Court appointment, but later decided against it after concluding that it might hurt his chances for the presidential nomination in 1848.

1847

April 15   Dispatched Nicholas P. Trist as peace commissioner to negotiate settlement of the war with Mexico.

December 25   Began a series of dinners which were given every ten days or so for the purpose of building up political fences in his quest for the 1848 presidential nomination.

1848

February 2   Treaty of Guadalupe Hidalgo was signed ending the war with Mexico in which the latter ceded New Mexico and California to the United States.

May   Democratic Convention again failed to nominate Buchanan for President. Lewis Cass of Michigan was selected.

December   Purchased Wheatland, a country estate near Lancaster. This became his permanent home.

1849

May   Took up residence in Wheatland after retiring from his cabinet position. Harriet Lane, a favorite niece, became hostess for all of Buchanan's social activities both in and out of public office.

1850

November 19 Opened his bid for the presidential nomination in 1852 with letter to a Democratic meeting expressing ambivalent opinion of the Compromise of 1850 bill recently passed by Congress. Expressed doubts that the popular sovereignty aspects of the provision would work, and favored strong enforcement of the Fugitive Slave Law which accompanied passage of Compromise Bill. This brought him Southern support.

1852

June   Democratic Party nominated Franklin Pierce as its candidate for President, thereby giving Buchanan his third disappointment in his pursuit of that nomination and office.

1853

Became President of the Board of Trustees of Franklin and Marshall College when these two previously separate institutions merged and situated themselves in Lancaster.

April 1   Invited by Pierce to accept appointment as envoy extraordinary and minister plenipotentiary to Great Britain.

August   Sailed for England, his main object being to get British recognition of the Monroe Doctrine.

First major "crisis" was his refusal to abide by the customary costume dress required by the Court Dress Circular. He wished to appear before her Majesty, Queen Victoria, in street clothes. Climaxed by a threat of a Parliamentary inquiry over his position in this matter, the situation was compromised by his agreement to wear a black-handled sword as a visible token of respect to the Queen.

1854

February 28 The Republican Party organized in Ripon, Wisconsin.

May 30	Kansas-Nebraska Act proposed by Stephen A. Douglas, signed by President Pierce.
October 18	Ostend Manifesto signed. Together with John Y. Mason, U.S. Minister to France, and Pierre Soulé, U.S. Minister to Spain, Buchanan declared at Ostend, Belgium, the purchase of Cuba from Spain, or if Spain refused to sell to take it by force. Its essential purpose was to secure more slave territory so that the episode brought favor to Buchanan in the South. Actually, however, the dispatch came from Aix-la-Chapelle, not from Ostend where the ministers originally met to draw up a policy.

1855

April	Requested that his mission to Great Britain be terminated and that he be recalled.
	During the course of the year he confided to friends that he was "available" for the presidential nomination in 1856.

1856

January15	Free State Party in Kansas, under Topeka Constitution, elected governor and legislature.
January 24	President Pierce recognized pro-slavery legislature in Territory of Kansas and condemned Topeka movement as revolutionary.
March 4	Topeka Legislature petitioned Congress for admission to the Union.
April 24	Arrived in New York on the *Arago* from his mission to England.
May 21	Civil war broke out in Kansas.
June 2	National Democratic Convention at Cincinnati nominated Buchanan for President and John C. Breckinridge of Kentucky as Vice-President.
November 4	Buchanan elected President. Polled 1,838,169 votes, while Frémont, Republican, polled 1,335,264, and Fillmore, the Whig and American (Know-Nothing) candidate, received 874,534. The Electoral College gave 174 votes to Buchanan, 114 to Fremont, and 8 to Fillmore.

December 29   Wrote a letter stating that, "The great object of my administration will be to arrest, if possible, the agitation of the slavery question at the North, and to destroy sectional parties. Should a kind Providence enable me to succeed in my efforts to restore harmony to the Union, I shall feel that I have not lived in vain."

TERM IN OFFICE
1857

March 4   Inaugurated as fifteenth president of the United States on the stand in front of the east portico of the Capitol in Washington. Chief Justice Roger Taney administered the oath of office. Legend had it that just before the swearing-in Taney whispered to Buchanan how the Supreme Court would decide the Dred Scott case, and that the President-elect thereupon immediately added this point to his inaugural speech. In truth, he knew about the decision a week before from one of the Justices, Robert C. Grier of Pennsylvania, and had urged Grier to support it. The Inaugural Address condemned slavery agitation, anticipated the Dred Scott decision, supported "popular sovereignty" in the Territories, and announced his intention to retire at the end of his term and under no circumstances seek re-election. His Cabinet consisted of: Lewis Cass of Michigan, Secretary of State; Howell Cobb of Georgia, Secretary of Treasury; John B. Floyd of Virginia, Secretary of War; Jeremiah S. Black of Pennsylvania, Attorney General; Aaron V. Brown of Tennessee, Postmaster General; Isaac Toucey of Connecticut, Secretary of Navy; Jacob Thompson of Mississippi, Secretary of Interior.

March 6   Dred Scott decision rendered by the Supreme Court. Among other things, this decision laid down the doctrine that the Fifth Amendment guaranteed the right of slaveholders to take their property into any of the territories, and so held that the Missouri Compromise was unconstitutional.

March 26   Robert J. Walker of Mississippi accepted Buchanan's appointment of him as governor of the territory of Kansas following the resignation of John W. Geary.

August 24   The New York Stock Exchange collapsed and the Panic of 1857 began, resulting in economic distress throughout the nation.
The Impending Crisis of the South: How To Meet It, published. This attack on the institution of slavery played an important part in the politics of the period.

September 11   Mountain Meadows Massacre in Utah Territory. Buchanan ordered the removal of Brigham Young as governor of Utah.

October 19   Lecompton convention convened for the purpose of writing a constitution for Kansas.

December 8   Delivered his First Annual Message to Congress, calling for relief rather than reform in response to economic distress; asked Congress to authorize use of federal troops to "reassert" federal authority in Utah; affirmed the legality of the Lecompton Constitution in Kansas.

December 17   Robert J. Walker resigned as Governor of Kansas after Buchanan failed to support him in the face of his Southern-dominated Cabinet's opposition to Walker who opposed the Lecompton Constitution providing for protection of existing slave property in Kansas and requiring a vote only on the question whether the Constitution should be adopted with or without slavery.

December 21   Lecompton Constitution with slavery voted in election, but Free State men did not participate.

1858

January 4   Lecompton Constitution rejected on second vote in Kansas Territory, with Free-State men voting.

January 7   Delivered a special message to Congress on the arrest of William Walker in Nicaragua, deploring "private invasions" in Central America which placed the United States government in a bad light in that area.

January 11   Submitted to Congress the constitution of the Territory of Minnesota which had been approved by the voters in that territory.

January 12	Named Nathan Clifford of Maine Associate Justice of the Supreme Court to fill vacancy caused by the resignation of Benjamin Robbins Curtis. This was the only Court appointment made by Buchanan.
February 2	Submitted the Lecompton Constitution to Congress, recommending the admission of Kansas as a slave state.
February 25	Issued a Proclamation abolishing discriminating duties in the case of the Papal States.
March 23	Senate voted to admit Kansas as a state under the Lecompton Constitution.
April 1	John J. Crittenden of Kentucky proposed re-submission of Lecompton Constitution to popular vote. Passed in the House of Representatives.
April 6	Issued a proclamation on the rebellion in Utah calling for use of military force to enforce the acts of federal officials.
April 30	William H. English of Indiana drew up compromise measure providing for popular vote on Lecompton which offered immediate admission of Kansas plus a large land grant if constitution accepted. Passed both Houses of Congress.
May 11	Minnesota entered the Union as a state.
June 10	Advised Congress that "our difficulties with the Territory of Utah have terminated, and the reign of the Constitution and the laws have been restored."
June 16	Abraham Lincoln nominated as Republican candidate for Senator from Illinois.
June 18	Treaty of peace, amity and commerce concluded with China.
July 29	Treaty with Japan which became basis for Japan's trade relations with foreign powers for rest of the century was completed by Townsend Harris.
August 3	Lecompton Constitution, submitted for the third time, rejected by Kansas voters, 11,812—1,962.

August 16   Queen Victoria and Buchanan exchanged greetings over the new Atlantic Cable.

August 21   Lincoln-Douglas debates began; slavery in the territories a major issue.

October 30   Issued Proclamation concerning an expedition against Nicaragua by private United States citizens, enjoining all government officials to suppress such activities and "exhorting all good citizens" to co-operate.

December 6   Second Annual Message to Congress asked for authority to establish a "temporary protectorate" over northern portions of Chihuahua and Sonora in Mexico. Senate later refused to approve proposal. Also urged the purchase of Cuba and the construction of a Pacific Railroad.

1859

February 14   Oregon admitted as 33rd state.

February 24   Vetoed a bill "donating public lands to the several States and Territories which may provide colleges for the benefit of agriculture and the mechanic arts." Buchanan considered the measure "inexpedient and unconstitutional"— further reflecting his narrow and strict construction of the Constitution.

March 8   Aaron V. Brown, Postmaster General, died.

March 14   Joseph Holt of Kentucky appointed Postmaster General.

May 12   The Vicksburg (Virginia) Commercial Convention adopted a resolution calling for the reopening of African slave trade. Buchanan opposed this.

July 29   Kansas constitutional convention at Wyandotte completed with provision prohibiting slavery.

October 4   Wyandotte Constitution ratified in Kansas Territory by popular vote.

October 16   John Brown raided Harpers Ferry and slavery issue became more inflamed than ever.

October 27	Third Annual Message to Congress dealt with Harpers Ferry incident, asserted that slavery in the territories was protected, that he as President could take no military action to protect federal authority without Congressional sanction, and that Congress had paralyzed the government by refusing to pass deficiency bills.

1860

February	Made strong statement that he would not be a candidate for re-election.
March	Delivered Special Message on the Covode Investigation defending himself against charges leveled by witnesses at hearings. Protested creation of such a committee for the purpose of investigating whether the President had, "by money, patronage, or any committee thereof, for or against the passage of any law appertaining to the rights of any State or Territory."
April 8	First run of Pony Express between St. Joseph, Missouri, and San Francisco.
April 11	Bill to admit Kansas with Wyandotte Constitution passed by House, but no action by Senate.
May 14	Japan's first diplomat to a foreign state received in Washington.
May 16	Republican National Convention in Chicago nominated Abraham Lincoln for President and Hannibal Hamlin of Maine for Vice-President.
June 22	Veto of the Homestead Bill brought great unpopularity to Democratic Party and probably contributed to the Republican victory of Lincoln later in the year.
June 23	Democratic Party Convention in Baltimore nominated Stephen A. Douglas of Illinois for President and Herschel V. Johnson of Georgia for Vice-President.
June 28	Southern seceders of the Democratic Party nominated Vice-President John C. Breckinridge of Kentucky for President and Joseph Lane of Oregon for Vice-President.

September	Held a grand state dinner in honor of the Prince of Wales who was touring Canada and the United States.
November 6	Abraham Lincoln elected President.
November 9	Buchanan called a special Cabinet meeting to consider South Carolina's threat to leave the Union.
December 3	Fourth Annual Message to Congress stated that the South had no legal right to secede nor had the federal government any power to prevent it. He recommended an "explanatory" amendment to the Constitution on the subject of slavery.
December 10	Howell Cobb, Secretary of Treasury, resigned to urge secession.
December 12	Philip F. Thomas of Maryland appointed Secretary of Treasury. Lewis Cass resigned as Secretary of State in protest of what he believed to be Buchanan's failure to deal strongly with the threat to Fort Sumter's security as federal property.
December 17	Jeremiah S. Black of Pennsylvania became Secretary of State leaving his post as Attorney General.
December 18	Crittenden compromise plan proposed in Senate aimed at influencing Southern states to drop plans of secession.
December 20	Edwin M. Stanton of Pennsylvania became Attorney General. South Carolina seceded from the Union by vote of 169-0.
December 22	South Carolina appointed three Commissioners to lay ordinance of secession before Buchanan and Congress and to negotiate for delivery of forts and other federal property within the state.
December 26	Major Robert Anderson occupied Fort Sumter in Charleston Harbor.
December 27	News of Major Anderson's move reached Washington. Called cabinet meeting to discuss whether Anderson should withdraw. No action taken.

December 28 Held interview with South Carolina Commissioners as "private gentlemen."

December 29 John B. Floyd resigned as Secretary of War under suspicion of alleged conspiracy to defraud the government.

South Carolina Commissioners demanded that Buchanan immediately withdraw troops from Charleston Harbor.

December 30 South Carolina troops seized United States arsenal at Charleston.

December 31 Replied to South Carolina Commissioners that he would not remove federal troops.

1861

January 2 Decision made to send reinforcements to Fort Sumter.

January 5 Received word from Anderson that reinforcements not required. Ship arrived before Buchanan could stop expedition.

January 8 Sent Congress Special Message concerning relations with South Carolina. Policy here enunciated stated his program for the balance of his term: To defend public property, to avoid any provocative act, and to seek expression of public opinion outside Congress.

Secretary of Interior Jacob Thompson resigned in protest of expedition of troops to Fort Sumter.

January 9—
February 4 Secession of Mississippi, Florida, Alabama, Georgia, Louisiana, Texas.

January 18 Postmaster General Joseph Holt assumed duties of Secretary of War.

January 19 Virginia legislature adopted resolutions inviting delegates from all interested states to assemble in Washington on February 4 for the purpose of promoting peace.

January 28 Submitted the Virginia Resolutions to Congress with his enthusiastic endorsement.

January 29   Kansas entered the Union as a free state under the Wy-
                andotte Constitution.

February 4   Convention of delegates from six seceded states met in
                Montgomery, Alabama, to form provisional government.

                Virginia Peace Convention met in Washington.

February 8   Constitution for the Provisional Government of Confed-
                erate States adopted by Montgomery convention.

February 24   Abraham Lincoln made his first call on the White House.

February 28   Colorado Territory formed.

March 2   Nevada and Dakota Territories formed.

March 4   Lincoln inaugurated. He and Buchanan drive in procession
                from Willard's Hotel to the Capitol. Buchanan turned to
                Lincoln and said, "Sir, if you are as happy in entering
                the White House as I shall feel on returning to Wheat-
                land, you are a happy man indeed."

RETIREMENT

March 6   Arrived in Wheatland to begin period of retirement.

April 12   Fort Sumter attacked and Civil War began.

April 23   Celebrated 71st birthday, and had a severe bilious seizure
                —an illness suffered most of his life.

                Outbreak of war resulted in number of charges that his
                Administration was really responsible.

July 4   Lincoln delivered address which pointed to Buchanan's
                responsibility for the weakness of the Federal forces to
                withstand the initial Southern assault.

1862

July   Buchanan accused by abolition newspapers of attempting
                to persuade foreign governments to recognize the Con-
                federacy. Subjected to charges from many quarters seek-
                ing to establish his Administration as "treasonable."

                Completed draft of his book, *Mr. Buchanan's Adminis-
                tration on the Eve of the Rebellion,* which was aimed at
                defending his presidential policy before the war broke out.

1865

September 23   Admitted to communion in the Presbyterian Church.

1866

January   John Appleton, publisher, published *Mr. Buchanan's Administration on the Eve of the Rebellion.*

1868

May   Became seriously ill with a cold and other complications of old age.

June 1   Died at half-past eight on Monday morning. Buried in Lancaster.

DOCUMENTS

INAUGURAL ADDRESS
March 4, 1857

Buchanan was in fact a "minority President," having polled 1,838,169 votes as against a total of 2,209,798, cast for his two major opponents, Fillmore and Frémont. He began by stating that he would not seek another term, which weakened his influence at once, and then went on to lay down guides for domestic and foreign policy. But the essential theme recognized the slavery agitation crisis which threatened the perpetuity of the Union. In this address, Buchanan anticipates the Dred Scott decision which was delivered just two days later. Since he himself influenced the Court in the position it took in this case he was indeed in a position to do this. One of the Justices advised him in advance and he took the occasion to gather public support for it. The Kansas-Nebraska Act and the issues concerning it plagued the Buchanan Administration to its very end.

I appear before you this day to take the solemn oath "that I will faithfully execute the office of President of the United States, and will, to the best of my ability, preserve, protect and defend the Constitution of the United States."

In entering upon this great office I most humbly invoke the God of our fathers for wisdom and firmness to execute its high and responsible duties in such a manner as to restore harmony and ancient friendship among the people of the several States, and to preserve our free institutions throughout many generations. Convinced that I owe my election to the inherent love for the Constitution and the Union which still animates the hearts of the American people, let me earnestly ask their powerful support in sustaining all just measures calculated to perpetuate these, the richest political blessings which Heaven has ever bestowed upon any nation. Having determined not to become a candidate for re-election, I shall have no motive to influence my conduct in administering the Government except the desire ably and faithfully to serve my country and to live in the grateful memory of my countrymen.

We have recently passed through a presidential contest in which the passions of our fellow-citizens were excited to the highest degree by questions of deep and vital importance; but when the people proclaimed their will the tempest at once subsided and all was calm.

21

The voice of the majority, speaking in the manner prescribed by the Constitution, was heard, and instant submission followed. Our own country could alone have exhibited so grand and striking a spectacle of the capacity of man for self-government.

What a happy conception, then, was it for Congress to apply this simple rule, that the will of the majority shall govern, to the settlement of the question of domestic slavery in the Territories! Congress is neither "to legislate slavery into any Territory or State, nor to exclude it therefrom, but to leave the people thereof perfectly free to form and regulate their domestic institutions in their own way, subject only to the Constitution of the United States." As a natural consequence, Congress has also prescribed that, when the Territory of Kansas shall be admitted as a State, it "shall be received into the Union, with or without slavery, as their constitution may prescribe at the time of their admission."

A difference of opinion has arisen in regard to the point of time when the people of a Territory shall decide this question for themselves.

This is, happily, a matter of but little practical importance. Besides, it is a judicial question, which legitimately belongs to the Supreme Court of the United States, before whom it is now pending, and will, it is understood, be speedily and finally settled. To their decision, in common with all good citizens, I shall cheerfully submit, whatever this may be, though it has ever been my individual opinion that, under the Nebraska-Kansas Act, the appropriate period will be when the number of actual residents in the Territory shall justify the formulation of a constitution with a view to its admission as a State into the Union. But be this as it may, it is the imperative and indispensable duty of the Government of the United States to secure to every resident inhabitant the free and independent expression of his opinion by his vote. This sacred right of each individual must be preserved. That being acomplished, nothing can be fairer than to leave the people of a Terrtory free from all foreign interference, to decide their own destiny for themselves, subject only to the Constitution of the United States.

The whole Territorial question being thus settled upon the principle of popular sovereignty—a principle as ancient as free government itself—everything of a practical nature has been decided. No other question remains for adjustment; because all agree that, under the Constitution, slavery in the States is beyond the reach of any human power, except that of the respective States themselves wherein it exists. May we not, then, hope that the long agitation on this subject is approaching its end, and that the geographical parties to which it has given birth, so much dreaded by the Father of his Country. will speedily become extinct? Most happy will it be for the country when the public mind shall be diverted from this question to others of more pressing and practical importance. Throughout the whole progress of this agitation, which has scarcely known any intermission for more than twenty years, whilst it has been productive of no positive good to any human being, it has been the prolific source of great evils to the master, the slave, and to the whole country. It has alienated and estranged the people of the sister States from each other, and has even seriously endangered the very existence of the Union. Nor has the danger yet entirely ceased. Under our system there is a remedy for all mere political evils in the sound sense and sober judgment of the people. Time is a great corrective. Political subjects which but a few years ago excited and exasperated the public mind have passed away and are now nearly forgotten. But this question of domestic slavery is of far greater importance than any mere political question, because, should the agitation continue, it may eventually endanger the personal safety of a large portion of our countrymen where the institution exists. In that event, no form of government, however admirable in itself, and however productive of material benefits, can compensate for the loss of peace and domestic security around the family altar. Let every Union-loving man, therefore, exert his best influence to suppress this agitation, which, since the recent legislation of Congress, is without any legitimate object.

It is an evil omen of the times that men have undertaken to calculate the mere material value of the Union. Reasoned estimates have been presented of the pecuniary profits and local advantages which would result to different States and sections from its dissolution, and of the comparative injuries which such an event would inflict on other States and sections. Even descending to this law and narrow view of the mighty question, all such calculations are at fault. The bare reference to a single consideration will be conclusive on this point. We at present enjoy a free trade throughout our extensive and expanding country, such as the world has never witnessed. This trade is conducted on railroads and canals—on noble rivers and arms of the sea—which bind together the North and the South, the East and the West of our confederacy. Annihilate this trade, arrest its free progress by the geographical lines of jealous and hostile States, and you destroy the prosperity and onward march of the whole and every part, and involve all in one common ruin. But such considerations, important as they are in themselves, sink into significance when we reflect on the terrific evils which would result from disunion to every portion of the confederacy—to the North not more than to the South, to the East not more than to the West. These I shall not attempt to portray; because I feel an humble confidence that the kind Providence which inspired our fathers with wisdom to frame the most perfect form of Government and Union ever devised by man will not suffer it to perish until it shall have been peacefully instrumental, by its example, in the extension of Civil and religious liberty throughout the whole world.

Next in importance to the maintenance of the Constitution and the Union is the duty of preserving the government free from the taint, or even suspicion, of corruption. Public virtue is the vital spirit of republics;

and history shows that when this has decayed, and the love of money has usurped its place, although the forms of free government may remain for a season, the substance has departed forever.

Our present financial condition is without a parallel in history. No nation has ever before been embarrassed from too large a surplus in its treasury. This almost necessarily gives birth to extravagant legislation. It produces wild schemes of expenditure, and begets a race of speculators and jobbers, whose ingenuity is exerted in contriving and promoting expedients to obtain public money. The purity of official agents, whether rightfully or wrongfully, is suspected, and the character of the government suffers in the estimation of the people. This is in itself a very great evil.

The natural mode of relief from this embarrassment is to appropriate the surplus in the treasury to great national objects, for which a clear warrant can be found in the Constitution. Among these I might mention the extinguishment of the public debt, a reasonable increase in the navy, which is at present inadequate to the protection of our vast tonnage afloat, now greater than any nation, as well as to the defense of our extended seacoast.

It is beyond all questions the true principle, that no more revenue ought to be collected from the people than the amount necessary to defray the expenses of a wise, economical, and efficient administration of the Government. To reach this point it was necessary to resort to a modification of the tariff, and this has, I trust, been accomplished in such a manner as to do as little injury as may have been practicable to our domestic manufactures, especially those necessary for the defense of the country. Any discrimination against a particular branch, for the purpose of benefiting favored corporations, individuals, or interests, would have been unjust to the rest of the community, and inconsistent with that spirit of fairness and equality which ought to govern in the adjustment of a revenue tariff.

But the squandering of the public money sinks into comparative insignificance as a temptation to corruption when compared with the squandering of the public lands.

No nation in the tide of time has ever been blessed with so rich and noble an inheritance as we enjoy in the public lands. In administering this important trust, whilst it may be wise to grant portions of them for the improvement of the remainder, yet we should never forget that it is our cardinal policy to reserve these lands, as much as may be, for actual settlers, and this at moderate prices. We shall thus not only best promote the prosperity of the new States and Territories by furnishing them a hardy and independent race of honest and industrious citizens, but shall secure homes for our children and our children's children, as well as for those exiles from foreign shores who may seek in this country to improve their condition, and to enjoy the blessings of civil and religious liberty. Such emigrants have done much to promote the growth and prosperity of the country. They have proved faithful both in peace and war. After becoming citizens, they are entitled, under the Constitution and laws, to be placed on a perfect equality with native-born citizens, and in this character they should ever be kindly recognized.

The Federal Constitution is a grant from the States to Congress of certain specific powers, and the question whether this grant should be liberally or strictly construed has more or less divided political parties from the beginning. Without entering into the argument, I desire to state at the commencement of my Administration that long experience and observation have convinced me that a strict construction of the powers of the Government is the only true, as well as the only safe, theory of the Constitution. Whenever in our past history doubtful powers have been exercised by Congress, these have never failed to produce injurious and unhappy consequences. Many such instances might be adduced if this were the proper occasion. Neither is it necessary for the public sercice to strain the language of the Constitution, because all the great and useful powers required for a successful administration of the Government both in peace and in war, have been granted, either in express terms or by the plainest implication.

Whilst deeply convinced of these truths, I yet consider it clear that under the war-making power Congress may appropriate money towards the construction of a military road when this is absolutely necessary for the defence of any State or Territory of the Union against foreign invasion. Under the Constitution Congress has power "to declare war," "to raise and support armies," "to provide and maintain a navy," and to call forth the militia to "repel invasions." Thus endowed, in an ample manner, with the war-making power, the corresponding duty is required that "the United States shall protect each of them (the States) against invasion." Now, how is it possible to afford this protection to California and our Pacific possessions except by means of a military road through the Territories of the United States, over which men and munitions of war may be speedily transported from the Atlantic States to meet and to repel the invader? In the event of a war with a naval power much stronger than our own we should then have no other available access to the Pacific Coast, because such a power would instantly close the route across the isthmus of Central America. It is impossible to conceive that whilst the Constitution has expressly required Congress to defend all the States it should yet deny to them, by any fair construction, the only possible means by which one of these States can be defended. Besides, the Government, ever since its origin, has been in the constant practice of constructing military roads. It might also be wise to consider whether the love for the Union which now animates our fellow-citizens on the Pacific Coast may not be impaired by our neglect or refusal to provide for them, in their remote and isolated condition, the only means by which the power of the States on this side of the Rocky Mountains can reach them in sufficient time to "protect" them "against invasion." I forbear for the present from expressing an opinion as to the wisest and most economical mode in which the Government can lend its aid in accomplishing this great and necessary work. I believe that many of the difficulties in the way, which now appear formidable, will in a great degree vanish as soon as the nearest and best route shall have been satisfactorily ascertained.

It may be proper that on this occasion I should make some brief remarks in regard to our rights and duties as a member of the great family of nations. In our intercourse with them there are some plain principles, approved by our own experience, from which we should never depart. We ought to cultivate peace, commerce, and friendship with all nations, and this not merely as the best means of promoting our own material interests, but in a spirit of Christian benevolence towards our fellow-men, wherever their lot may be cast. Our diplomacy should be direct and frank, neither seeking to obtain more nor accepting less than is our due. We ought to cherish a sacred regard for the independence of all nations, and never attempt to interfere in the domestic concerns of any unless this shall be imperatively required by the great laws of self-preservation. To avoid entangling alliances has been a maxim of our policy ever since the days of Washington, and its wisdom no one will attempt to dispute. In short, we ought to do justice, in a kindly spirit to all nations and require justice from them in return.

It is our glory that, whilst other nations have extended their dominions by the sword we have never acquired any territory except by fair purchase or, as in the case of Texas, by the voluntary determination of a brave, kindred, and independent people to blend their destinies with our own. Even our acquisitions from Mexico form no exception. Unwilling to take advantage of the fortune of war against a sister republic, we purchased these possessions, under the treaty of peace, for a sum which was considered at the time a fair equivalent. Our past history forbids that we shall in the future acquire territory, unless this be sanctioned by the laws of justice and honor. Acting on this principle, no nation will have a right to interfere or to complain if in the progress of events we shall still further extend our possessions. Hitherto in all our acquisitions the people, under the protection of the American flag, have enjoyed civil and religious liberty, as well as equal and just laws, and have been contented, prosperous, and happy. Their trade with the rest of the world has rapidly increased, and thus every commercial nation has shared largely in their successful progress.

I shall now proceed to take the oath prescribed by the Constitution, whilst humbly invoking the blessing of Divine Providence on this great people.

FIRST ANNUAL MESSAGE
December 8, 1857

The economic Panic of 1857 and the crisis in Kansas were the main events which dominated the American setting at the outset of Buchanan's administration. Buchanan's first message on the "State of the Union" therefore dealt with the tensions and uncertainties caused by the political and economic turmoil of the period. While this lengthy document embraced so many topics, one stood out, and that was Kansas. The President related in detail the history of the Lecompton convention, and he was careful to make no recommendation as to whether Congress should accept the decision of the Kansans in their vote to include or exclude slavery. In the area of foreign relations, which takes on ever increasing importance in presidential administrations, much of Buchanan's attention is directed to Great Britain and her role in Latin-America.

Fellow-Citizens of the Senate and House of Representatives:

In obedience to the command of the Constitution, it has now become my duty "to give to Congress information of the state of the Union, and recommend to their consideration such measures" as I judge to be "necessary and expedient."

But first and above all, our thanks are due to Almighty God for the numerous benefits which He has bestowed upon this people, and our united prayers ought to ascend to Him that He would continue to bless our great Republic in time to come as He has blessed it in time past. Since the adjournment of the last Congress our constituents have enjoyed an unusual degree of health. The earth has yielded her fruits abundantly and has bountifully rewarded the toil of the husbandman. Our great staples have commanded high prices, and up till within a brief period our manufacturing, mineral, and mechanical occupations have largely partaken of the general prosperity. We have possessed all the elements of material wealth in rich abundance, and yet, notwithstanding all these

advantages, our country in its monetary interests is at the present moment in a deplorable condition. In the midst of unsurpassed plenty in all the productions of agriculture and in all the elements of national wealth, we find our manufactures suspended, our public works retarded, our private enterprises of different kinds abandoned, and thousands of useful laborers thrown out of employment and reduced to want. The revenue of the Government, which is chiefly derived from duties on imports from abroad, has been greatly reduced, whilst the appropriations made by Congress at its last session for the current fiscal year are very large in amount.

Under these circumstances a loan may be required before the close of your present session; but this, although deeply to be regretted, would prove to be only a light misfortune when compared with the suffering and distress prevailing among the people. With this the Government cannot fail deeply to sympathize, though it may be without the power to extend relief.

It is our duty to inquire what has produced such unfortunate results and whether their recurrence can be prevented. In all former revulsions the blame might have been fairly attributed to a variety of co-operating causes, but not so upon the present occasion. It is apparent that our existing misfortunes have proceeded solely from our extravagant and vicious system of paper currency and bank credits, exciting the people to wild speculations and gambling in stocks. These revulsions must continue to recur at successive intervals so long as the amount of the paper currency and bank loans and discounts of the country shall be left to the discretion of fourteen hundred irresponsible banking institutions, which from the very law of their nature will consult the interest of their stockholders rather than the public welfare. . . .

. . . It is easy to account for our financial history for the last forty years. It has been a history of extravagant expansions in the business of the country, followed by ruinous contractions. At successive intervals the best and most enterprising men have been tempted to their ruin by excessive bank loans of mere paper credit, exciting them to extravagant importations of foreign goods, wild speculations, and ruinous and demoralizing stock gambling. When the crisis arrives, as arrive it must, the banks can extend no relief to the people. In a vain struggle to redeem their liabilities in specie they are compelled to contract their loans and their issues, and at last, in the hour of distress, when their assistance is most needed, they and their debtors together sink into insolvency.

It is this paper system of extravagant expansion, raising the nominal price of every article far beyond its real value when compared with the cost of similar articles in countries whose circulation is wisely regulated which has prevented us from competing in our own markets with foreign manufactures has produced extravagant importations, and has counter-

acted the effect of the large incidental protection afforded to our domestic manufactures by the present revenue tariff. But for this the branches of our manufactures composed of raw materials, the production of our own country—such as cotton, iron, and woolen fabrics—would not only have acquired almost exclusive possession of the home market, but would have created for themselves a foreign market throughout the world.

Deplorable, however, as may be our present financial condition, we may yet indulge in bright hopes for the future. No other nation has ever existed which could have endured such violent expansions and contractions of paper credits without lasting injury; yet the buoyancy of youth, the energies of our population, and the spirit which never quails before difficulties will enable us soon to recover from our present financial embarrassments, and may even occasion us speedily to forget the lesson which they have taught.

In the meantime it is the duty of the Government, by all proper means within its power, to aid in alleviating the sufferings of the people occasioned by the suspension of the banks and to provide against a recurrence of the same calamity. Unfortunately, in either aspect of the case it can do but little. Thanks to the independent treasury, the Government has not suspended payment, as it was compelled to do by the failure of the banks in 1837. It will continue to discharge its liabilities to the people in gold and silver. Its disbursements in coin will pass into circulation and materially assist in restoring a sound currency. From its high credit, should we be compelled to make a temporary loan, it can be effected on advantageous terms. This, however, shall if possible be a-voided, but if not, then the amount shall be limited to the lowest practicable sum.

I have therefore determined that whilst no useful Government works already in progress shall be suspended, new works not already commenced will be postponed if this can be done without injury to the country. Those necessary for its defense shall proceed as though there had been no crisis in our monetary affairs.

But the Federal Government cannot do much to provide against a recurrence of existing evils. Even if insurmountable constitutional objections did not exist against the creation of a national bank, this would furnish no adequate preventive security. The history of the last Bank of the United States abundantly proves the truth of this assertion. . . .

After all, we must mainly rely upon the patriotism and wisdom of the States for the prevention and redress of the evil. . . .

Congress, in my opinion, possesses the power to pass a uniform bankrupt law applicable to all banking institutions throughout the United States, and I strongly recommend its exercise. This would make it the irreversible organic law of each bank's existence that a suspension of specie payments shall produce its civil death. The instinct of self-preservation would then compel it to perform its duties in such a manner as to escape the penalty and preserve its life.

The existence of banks and the circulation of bank paper are so identified with the habits of our people that they cannot at this day be suddenly abolished without much immediate injury to the country. If we could confine them to their appropriate sphere and prevent them from administering to the spirit of wild and reckless speculation by extravagant loans and issues, they might be continued with advantage to the public.

But this I say, after long and much reflection: If experience shall prove it to be impossible to enjoy the facilities which well-regulated banks might afford without at the same time suffering the calamities which the excesses of the banks have hitherto inflicted upon the country, it would then be far the lesser evil to deprive them altogether of the power to issue a paper currency and confine them to the functions of banks of deposit and discount.

Our relations with foreign governments are upon the whole in a satisfactory condition.

The diplomatic difficulties which existed between the Government of the United States and that of Great Britain at the adjournment of the last Congress have been happily terminated by the appointment of a British minister to this country, who has been cordially received.

Whilst it is greatly to the interest, as I am convinced it is the sincere desire, of the Governments and people of the two countries to be on terms of intimate friendship with each other, it has been our misfortune almost always to have had some irritating, if not dangerous, outstanding question with Great Britain.

Since the origin of the Government we have been employed in negotiating treaties with that power, and afterwards in discussing their true intent and meaning. In this respect the convention of April 19, 1850, commonly called the Clayton and Bulwer treaty, has been the most unfortunate of all because the two Governments place directly opposite and contradictory constructions upon its first and most important article. Whilst in the United States we believed that this treaty would place both powers upon an exact equality by the stipulation that neither will ever "occupy, or fortify, or colonize, or assume or exercise any dominion" over any part of Central America, it is contended by the British Government that the true construction of this language has left them in the rightful possession of all that portion of Central America which was in their occupancy at the date of the treaty; in fact, that the treaty is a virtual recognition on the part of the United States of the right of Great Britain, either as owner or protector, to the whole extensive coast of Central America, sweeping round from the Rio Hondo to the port and harbor of San Juan de Nicaragua, together with the adjacent Bay Islands, except the comparatively small portion of this between the Sarstoon and Cape Honduras. According to their construction, the treaty does no more than simply prohibit them from extending their possessions in Central America beyond the present limits. It is not too much to assert that if in the United States the treaty had been considered susceptible of such a construction it never would have been negotiated under the authority of the President, nor would it have received the approbation of the Senate. The universal conviction in the United States was that when our Government consented to violate its traditional and time-honored policy, and to stipulate with a foreign government never to occupy or acquire territory in the Central American portion of our own continent, the consideration for this sacrifice was that Great Britain should, in this respect at least, be placed in the same position with ourselves. Whilst we have no right to doubt the sincerity of the British government in their construction of the treaty, it is at the same time my deliberate conviction that this construction is in opposition both to its letter and its spirit. . . .

The British government, immediately after rejecting the treaty as amended, proposed to enter into a new treaty with the United States, similar in all respects to the treaty which they had just refused to ratify, if the United States would consent to add to the Senate's clear and unqualified recognition of the sovereignty of Honduras over the Bay Islands the following conditional stipulation: "Whenever and so soon as the Republic of Honduras shall have concluded and ratified a treaty with Great Britain by which Great Britain shall have ceded and the Republic of Honduras shall have accepted the said islands, subject to the provisions and conditions contained in such treaty."

This proposition was, of course, rejected. After the Senate had refused to recognize the British convention with Honduras of the 27th August, 1856, with full knowledge of its contents, it was impossible for me, necessarily ignorant of "the provisions and conditions" which might be contained in a future convention between the same parties, to sanction them in advance.

The fact is that when two nations like Great Britain and the United States, mutually desirous, as they are, and I trust ever may be, of maintaining the most friendly relations with each other, having unfortunately concluded a treaty which they understand in senses directly opposite, the wisest course is to abrogate such a treaty by mutual consent and to commence anew. . . . The interest of the two countries in Central America is identical, being confined to securing safe transits over all the routes across the Isthmus.

Whilst entertaining these sentiments, I shall, nevertheless, not refuse to contribute to any reasonable adjustment of the Central American questions which is not practically inconsistent with the American interpretation of the treaty. Overtures for this purpose have been recently made by the

British government in a friendly spirit, which I cordially reciprocate, but whether this renewed effort will result in success I am not yet prepared to express an opinion. A brief period will determine.

With France our ancient relations of friendship still continue to exist. . . . It is, nothwithstanding, much to be regretted that two nations whose productions are of such a character as to invite the most extensive exchanges and freest commercial intercourse should continue to enforce ancient and obsolete restrictions of trade against each other. Our commercial treaty with France is in this respect an exception from our treaties with all other commercial nations. It jealously levies discriminating duties both on tonnage and on articles the growth, produce, or manufacture of the one country when arriving in vessels belonging to the other. . . . Let us hope that this exception may not long exist.

Our relations with Russia remain, as they have ever been, on the most friendly footing. The present Emperor, as well as his predecessors, have never failed when the occasion offered to manifest their good will to our country, and their friendship has alwasy been highly appreciated by the Government and people of the United States.

With all other European governments, except that of Spain, our relations are as peaceful as we could desire. I regret to say that no progress whatever has been made since the adjournment of Congress towards the settlement of any of the numerous claims of our citizens against the Spanish Government. Besides, the outrage committed on our flag by the Spanish war-frigate *Ferrolana* on the high seas off the coast of Cuba in March, 1855, by firing into the American mail steamer *El Dorado,* and detaining and searching her, remains unacknowledged and unredressed. The general tone and temper of the Spanish Government toward that of the United States are much to be regretted. Our present envoy extraordinary and minister plenipotentiary to Madrid has asked to be recalled, and it is my purpose to send out a new minister to Spain with special instructions on all questions pending between the two Governments, and with a determination to have them speedily and amicably adjusted if this be possible. . .

A treaty of friendship and commerce was concluded at Constantinople on the 13th December, 1856, between the United States and Persia. . . . This treaty, it is believed, will prove beneficial to American commerce. The Shah has manifested an earnest disposition to cultivate friendly relations with our country, and has expressed a strong wish that we should be represented at Teheran by a minister plenipotentiary; and I recommend that an appropriation be made for this purpose.

Recent occurrences in China have been unfavorable to a revision of the treaty with that Empire of the 3d July, 1844, with a view to the security and extension of our commerce. . . . This was suspended by the occurrence of hostilities in the Canton River between Great Britain and the Chinese Empire. These hostilities have necessarily interrupted the trade of all nations with Canton, which is now in a state of blockade, and have occasioned a serious loss of life and property. Meanwhile the insurrection within the Empire against the existing imperial dynasty still continues, and it is difficult to anticipate what will be the result. . . .

Whilst our minister has been instructed to occupy a neutral position in reference to the existing hostilities at Canton, he will cordially co-operate with the British and French ministers in all peaceful measures to secure by treaty stipulations those just concessions to commerce which the nations of the world have a right to expect and which China cannot long be permitted to withhold. From assurances I have received I entertain no doubt that the three ministers will act in harmonious concert to obtain similar commercial treaties for each of the powers they represent.

We cannot fail to feel a deep interest in all that concerns the welfare of the independent Republics on our own continent, as well as of the Empire of Brazil. . . .

It is one of the first and highest duties of any independent state in its relations with the members of the great family of nations to restrain its people from acts of hostile aggression against their citizens or subjects. The most eminent writers on public law do not hesitate to denounce such hostile acts as robbery and murder.

Weak and feeble states like those of Central America, may not feel themselves able to assert and vindicate their rights. The case would be far different if expeditions were set on foot within our own territories to make private war against a powerful nation. If such expeditions were fitted out from abroad against any portion of our own country, to burn down our cities, murder and plunder our people, and usurp our Government, we should call any power on earth to the strictest account for not preventing such enormities.

When it was first rendered probable that an attempt would be made to get up another unlawful expedition against Nicaragua, the Secretary of State issued instructions to the marshals and district attorneys, which were directed by the Secretaries of War and the Navy to the appropriate army and navy officers, requiring them to be vigilant and to use their best exertions in carrying into effect the provisions of the act of 1818. Notwithstanding these precautions, the expedition has escaped from our shores. Such enterprises can do no possible good to the country, but have already inflicted much injury both on its interests and its character. They have prevented peaceful emigration from the United States to the States of Central America, which could not fail to prove highly beneficial to all the parties concerned. In a pecuniary point of view alone our citizens have sustained heavy losses from the seizure and closing of the transit route by the San Juan between the two oceans.

The leader of the recent expedition was arrested at New Orleans, but was discharged on giving bail for his appearance in the insufficient sum of $2,000.

I commend the whole subject to the serious attention of Congress, believing that our duty and our interest, as well as our national character, require that we should adopt such measures as will be effectual in restraining our citizens from committing such outrages.

I regret to inform you that the President of Paraguay has refused to ratify the treaty between the United States and that State as amended by the Senate, the signature of which was mentioned in the message of my predecessor to Congress at the opening of its session in December, 1853. The reasons assigned for this refusal will appear in the correspondence herewith submitted. . . .

Citizens of the United States also who were established in business in Paraguay have had their property seized and taken from them, and have otherwise been treated by the authorities in an insulting and arbitrary manner, which requires redress.

A demand for these purposes will be made in a firm but conciliatory spirit. This will the more probably be granted if the Executive shall have authority to use other means in the event of a refusal. This is accordingly recommended.

It is unnecessary to state in detail the alarming condition of the Territory of Kansas at the time of my inauguration. The opposing parties then stood in hostile array against each other, and any accident might have relighted the flames of civil war. Besides, at this critical moment Kansas was left without a governor by the resignation of Governor Geary.

On the 19th of February previous the Territorial legislature had passed a law providing for the election of delegates on the third Monday of June to a convention to meet on the first Monday of September for the purpose of framing a constitution preparatory to admission into the Union.

This law was in the main fair and just, and it is to be regretted that all the qualified electors had not registered themselves and voted under its provisions.

At the time of the election for delegates, an extensive organization existed in the Territory whose avowed object it was, if need be, to put down the lawful government by force and to establish a government of their own under the so-called Topeka constitution. The persons attached to this revolutionary organization abstained from taking any part in the election.

The act of the Territorial legislature had omitted to provide for submitting to the people the constitution which might be framed by the convention, and in the excited state of public feeling throughout Kansas an apprehension extensively prevailed that a design existed to force upon them a constitution in relation to slavery against their will. In this emergency it became my duty, as it was my unquestionable right, having in view the union of all good citizens in support of the Territorial laws, to express an opinion on the true construction of the provisions concerning slavery contained in the organic act of Congress of the 30th May, 1854. Congress declared it to be "the true intent and meaning of this act not to legislate slavery into any Territory or State, nor to exclude it therefrom, but to leave the people thereof perfectly free to form and regulate their domestic institutions in their own way." Under it Kansas, "when admitted as a State," was to "be received into the Union with or without slavery, as their constitution may prescribe at the time of their admission."

Did Congress mean by this language that the delegates elected to frame a constitution should have authority finally to decide the question of slavery, or did they intend by leaving it to the people that the people of Kansas themselves should decide this question by a direct vote? On this subject I confess I had never entertained a serious doubt, and therefore in my instructions to Governor Walker of the 28th March last I merely said that when "a constitution shall be submitted to the people of the Territory they must be protected in the exercise of their right of voting for or against that instrument, and the fair expression of the popular will must not be interrupted by fraud or violence."

In expressing this opinion it was far from my intention to interfere with the decision of the people of Kansas, either for or against slavery. From this I have always abstained. Instrusted with the duty of taking "care that the laws be faithfully executed," my only desire was that the people of Kansas should furnish to Congress the evidence required by the organic act, whether for or against slavery, and in this manner smooth their passage into the Union. In emerging from the condition of territorial dependence into that of a sovereign State it was their duty, in my opinion, to make known their will by the votes of the majority on the direct question whether this important domestic institution should or should not continue to exist. Indeed, this was the only possible mode in which their will could be authentically ascertained. . . .

The convention to frame a constitution for Kansas met on the first Monday of September last. They were called together by virtue of an act of the Territorial legislature, whose lawful existence had been recognized by Congress in different forms and by different enactments. A large proportion of the citizens of Kansas did not think proper to register their names and to vote at the election for delegates; but an opportunity to do this having been fairly afforded, their refusal to avail themselves of their right could in no manner affect the legality of the convention.

This convention proceeded to frame a constitution for Kansas, and finally adjourned on the 7th day of November. But little difficulty occurred in the convention except on the subject of slavery. The truth is that the general provisions of our recent State constitutions are so similar and, I may add, so excellent that the difference between them is not essential. Under the earlier practice of the Government no constitution

framed by the convention of a Territory preparatory to its admission
into the Union as a State had been submitted to the people. I trust,
however, the example set by the last Congress, requiring that the constitution of Minnesota "should be subject to the approval and ratification
of the people of the proposed State," may be followed on future occasions. I took it for granted that the convention of Kansas would act in
accordance with this example, founded as it is, on correct principles,
and hence my instructions to Governor Walker in favor of submitting
the constitution to the people were expressed in general and unqualified
terms.

In the Kansas-Nebraska act, however, this requirement, as applicable
to the whole constitution, had not been inserted, and the convention
were not bound by its terms to submit any other portion of the instrument to an election except that which relates to the "domestic institution" of slavery. This will be rendered clear by a simple reference to its
language. It was "not to legislate slavery into any Territory or State,
nor to exclude it therefrom, but to leave the people thereof perfectly
free to form and regulate their domestic institutions in their own way."
According to the plain construction of the sentence, the words "domestic institutions" have a direct, as they have an appropriate, reference to
slavery. "Domestic institutions" are limited to the family. The relation
between master and slave and a few others are "domestic institutions,"
and are entirely distinct from institutions of a political character. Besides, there was no question then before Congress, nor, indeed has there
since been any serious question before the people of Kansas or the
country, except that which relates to the "domestic institution" of slavery.

The convention, after an angry and excited debate, finally determined,
by a majority of only two, to submit the question of slavery to the
people, though at the last forty-three of the fifty delegates present affixed
their signatures to the constitution.

A large majority of the convention were in favor of establishing slavery
in Kansas. They accordingly inserted an article in the constitution for this
purpose similar in form to those which had been adopted by other Territorial conventions. In the schedule, however, providing for the transition
from a Territorial to a State government the question has been fairly and
explicit referred to the people whether they will have a constitution
"with or without slavery." It declares that before the constitution adopted
by the convention "shall be sent to Congress for admission into the
Union as a State" an election shall be held to decide this question, at
which all the white male inhabitants of the Territory above the age of
21 are entitled to vote. They are to vote by ballot, and "the ballots cast
at said election shall be endorsed 'constitution with slavery,' and 'constitution with no slavery.' " If there be a majority in favor of the "constitution with slavery," then it is to be transmitted to Congress by the
President of the Convention in its original form; if, on the contrary,

there shall be a majority in favor of the "constitution with no slavery," "then the article providing for slavery shall be stricken from the constitution by the president of this convention;" and it is expressly declared that "no slavery shall exist in the State of Kansas, except that the right of property in slaves now in the Territory shall in no manner be interfered with;" and in that event it is made his duty to have the constitution thus ratified transmitted to the Congress of the United States for the admission of the State into the Union.

At this election every citizen will have an opportunity of expressing his opinion by his vote "whether Kansas shall be received into the Union with or without slavery," and thus this exciting question may be peacefully settled in the very mode required by the organic law. The election will be held under legitimate authority, and if any portion of the inhabitants shall refuse to vote, a fair opportunity to do so having been presented, this will be their own voluntary act and they alone will be responsible for the consequences.

Whether Kansas shall be a free or slave State must eventually, under some authority, be decided by an election; and the question can never be more clearly or distinctly presented to the people than it is at the present moment. Should this opportunity be rejected she may be involved for years in domestic discord and possibly in civil war, before she can again make up the issue now so fortunately tendered and again reach the point she has already attained.

Kansas has for some years occupied too much of the public opinion. It is high time this should be directed to far more important objects. When once admitted into the Union, whether with or without slavery, the excitement beyond her own limits will speedily pass away, and she will then for the first time be left, as she ought to have been long since, to manage her own affairs in her own way. If her constitution on the subject of slavery or on any other subject be displeasing to a majority of the people, no human power can prevent them from changing it within a brief period. Under these circumstances it may well be questioned whether the peace and quiet of the whole country are not of greater importance than the mere temporary triumph of either of the political parties in Kansas.

Should the constitution without slavery be adopted by the votes of the majority, the rights of property in slaves now in the Territory are reserved. The number of these is very small, but if it were greater the provision would be equally just and reasonable. The slaves were brought into the Territory under the Constitution of the United States and are now the property of their masters. This point has at length been finally decided by the highest judicial tribunal of the country, and this upon the plain principle that when a confederacy of sovereign States acquire a new territory at their joint expense, both equality and justice demand that the citizens of one and all of them shall have the right to take into it whatsoever is recognized as property by the common Constitution. To have summarily confiscated the property in slaves already in the Territory would have been an act of gross injustice and contrary to the practice of the older States of the Union which have abolished slavery.

A Territorial government was established for Utah by act of Congress approved the 9th September, 1850, and the Constitution and laws of the United States were thereby extended over it "so far as the same or any provisions thereof may be applicable." This act provided for the appointment by the President, by and with the advice and consent of the Senate, of a governor . . . Brigham Young was appointed the first governor on the 20th September, 1850, and has held the office ever since. Whilst Governor Young has been both governor and superintendent of Indian affairs throughout this period he has been at the same time the head of the church called the Latter-day Saints, and professes to govern its members and dispose of their property by direct inspiration and authority from the Almighty. His power has been, therefore, absolute over both church and state.

The people of Utah almost exclusively belong to this church, and believing with a fanatical spirit that he is governor of the Territory by divine appointment, they obey his commands as if these were direct revelations from Heaven. If, therefore, he chooses that his government shall come into collision with the Government of the United States, the members of the Mormon church will yield implicit obedience to his will. Unfortunately, existing facts leave but little doubt that such is his determination. Without entering upon a minute history of occurrences, it is sufficient to say that all the officers of the United States, judicial and executive, with the single exception of two Indian agents, have found it necessary for their own personal safety to withdraw from the Territory, and there no longer remains any government in Utah but the despotism of Brigham Young. This being the condition of affairs in the Territory, I could not mistake the path of duty. As Chief Executive Magistrate I was bound to restore the supremacy of the Constitution and laws within its limits. In order to effect this purpose, I appointed a new governor and other federal officers for Utah and sent with them a military force for their protection, and to aid as a *posse comitatus* in case of need in the execution of the laws. . . .

No wise government will lightly estimate the efforts which may be inspired by such frenzied fanaticism as exists among the Mormons in Utah. This is the first rebellion which has existed in our Territories; and humanity itself requires that we should put it down in such a manner that it shall be the last. . . .

I recommend to Congress the establishment of a Territorial government over Arizona, incorporating with it such portions of New Mexico as they may deem expedient. . . . The proposed Territory is believed to be rich in mineral and agricultural resources, especially in silver and copper. . . .

Long experience has deeply convinced me that a strict construction of the powers granted to Congress is the only true, as well as the only safe, theory of the Constitution. Whilst this principle shall guide my public conduct, I consider it clear that under the war-making power Congress may appropriate money for the construction of a military road through the Territories of the United States when this is absolutely necessary for the defense of any of the States against foreign invasion. . . . Without such a road it is quite evident we cannot "protect" California and our Pacific possessions "against invasion." We cannot by any other means transport men and munitions of war from the Atlantic States in sufficient time successfully to defend these remote and distant portions of the Republic. . . .

The difficulties and expense of constructing a military railroad to connect our Atlantic and Pacific States have been greatly exaggerated. . . .

For obvious reasons the Government ought not to undertake the work itself by means of its own agents. This ought to be committed to other agencies, which Congress might assist, either by grants of land or money, or by both, upon such terms and conditions as they may deem most beneficial for the country. Provision might thus be made not only for the safe, rapid, and economical transportation of troops and minitions of war, but also of the public mails. The commercial interests of the whole country both East and West, would be greatly promoted by such a road, and, above all, it would be a powerful additional bond of union. . . . For these reasons I commend to the friendly consideration of Congress the subject of the Pacific railroad, without finally committing myself to any particular route. . . .

I transmit herewith the reports made to me by the Secretaries of War, of the Navy, and of the Interior, and the Post-master General. They all contain valuable and important information and suggestions, which I commend to the favorable consideration of Congress. . . .

It ought ever to be our cardinal policy to reserve the public lands as much as may be possible for actual settlers, and this at moderate prices. We shall thus not only best promote the prosperity of the new States and Territories, and the power of the Union, but shall secure homes for our posterity for many generations. . . .

JAMES BUCHANAN

SECOND ANNUAL MESSAGE
December 6, 1858

At a state constitutional convention at Lecompton, Kansas, in October, 1857, pro-slavery delegates named in a rigged election not only wrote a constitution explicitly guaranteeing slavery, but further refused to permit the electorate as a whole to vote on it. Under pressure, however, they did offer the electorate a proposition which restricted the entry of new slaves but which protected slave property already in the state. The majority anti-slavery voters refused to participate in the balloting on this proposition and the pro-slavery party thereby prevailed. In his Annual Message Buchanan explains why he would be duty bound to transmit the Kansas constitution to Congress, no matter which one the voters chose. The position of the United States in the hostilities between Great Britain and France on the one side, and China on the other, is one of the important issues of the period. The "complications" continuing between Great Britain and the United States over Britain's activities in Central America still plagues Buchanan's administration.

Fellow-Citizens of the Senate and House of Representatives:

When we compare the condition of the country at the present day with what it was one year ago at the meeting of Congress, we have much reason for gratitude to that Almighty Providence which has never failed to interpose for our relief at the most critical periods of our history. One year ago the sectional strife between the North and the South on the dangerous subject of slavery had again become so intense as to threaten the peace and perpetuity of the Confederacy. The application for the admission of Kansas as a State into the Union fostered this unhappy agitation and brought the whole subject once more before

Congress. It was the desire of every patriot that such measures of legislation might be adopted as would remove the excitement from the States and confine it to the Territory where it legitimately belonged. Much has been done, I am happy to say, towards the accomplishment of this object during the last session of Congress. . . .

During the session of 1856 much of the time of Congress was occupied on the question of admitting Kansas under the Topeka constitution. Again, nearly the whole of the last session was devoted to the question of its admission under the Lecompton constitution. Surely it is not unreasonable to require the people of Kansas to wait before making a third attempt until the number of their inhabitants shall amount to 93,420. During this brief period the harmony of the States as well as the great business interests of the country demands that the people of the Union shall not for a third time be convulsed by another agitation on the Kansas question. By waiting for a short time and acting in obedience to law Kansas will glide into the Union without the slightest impediment.

This excellent provision, which Congress has applied to Kansas, ought to be extended and rendered applicable to all Territories which may hereafter seek admission into the Union. . . .

I earnestly recommend the passage of a general act which shall provide that, upon the application of a Territorial legislature declaring their belief that the Territory contains a number of inhabitants which, if in a State, would entitle them to elect a member of Congress, it shall be the duty of the President to cause a census of the inhabitants to be taken, and if found sufficient then by the terms of this act to authorize them to proceed "in their own way" to frame a State constitution preparatory to admission into the Union. I also recommend that an appropriation may be made to enable the President to take a census of the people of Kansas.

The present condition of the Territory of Utah, when contrasted with what it was one year ago, is a subject for congratulation. It was then in a state of open rebellion, and, cost what it might, the character of the Government required that this rebellion should be suppressed and the Mormons compelled to yield obedience to the Constitution and the laws. In order to accomplish this object, as I informed you in my last annual message, I appointed a new governor instead of Brigham Young, and other Federal officers to take the place of those who, consulting their personal safety, had found it necessary to withdraw from the Territory. To protect these civil officers, and to aid them, as a *posse comitatus,* in the execution of the laws in case of need, I ordered a detachment of the Army to accompany them to Utah. The necessity for adopting these measures is now demonstrated.

I am happy to inform you that the governor and other civil officers of Utah are now performing their appropriate functions without resistance. The authority of the Constitution and the laws has been fully restored, and peace prevails throughout the Territory.

I have occasion, also, to congratulate you on the result of our negotiations with China.

You were informed by my last annual message that our minister had been instructed to occupy a neutral position in the hostilities conducted by Great Britain and France against Canton. He was, however, at the same time directed to co-operate cordially with the British and French ministers in all peaceful measures to secure by treaty those just concessions to foreign commerce which the nations of the world had a right to demand. It was impossible for me to proceed further than this on my own authority without usurping the war-making power, which, under the Constitution belongs exclusively to Congress.

The event has proved the wisdom of our neutrality. Our minister has executed his instructions with eminent skill and ability. In conjunction with the Russian plenipotentiary, he has peacefully, but effectually, co-operated with the English and French plenipotentiaries, and each of the four powers has concluded a separate treaty with China of a highly satisfactory character. The treaty concluded by our own plenipotentiary will immediately be submitted to the Senate.

I am happy to announce that through the energetic yet conciliatory efforts of our consul general in Japan, a new treaty has been concluded with that Empire, which may be expected materially to augment our trade and intercourse in that quarter and remove from our countrymen the disabilities which have heretofore been imposed upon the exercise of their religion. The treaty shall be submitted to the Senate for approval without delay.

It is my earnest desire that every misunderstanding with the Government of Great Britain should be amicably and speedily adjusted. It has been the misfortune of both countries, almost ever since the period of the Revolution, to have been annoyed by a succession of irritating and dangerous questions, threatening their friendly relations. This has partially prevented the full development of those feelings of mutual friendship between the people of the two countries so natural in themselves and so conducive to their common interest. Any serious interruption of the commerce between the United States and Great Britain would be equally injurious to both. In fact, no two nations have ever existed on the face of the earth which could do each other so much good or so much harm. Entertaining these sentiments, I am gratified to inform you that the long-pending controversy between the two Governments, in relation to the question of visitation and search has been amicably adjusted. The claim on the part of Great Britain forcibly to visit American vessels on the high seas in time of peace could not be sustained under the law of nations, and it had been overruled by her own most eminent jurists.

I am truly sorry I cannot also inform you that the complications between Great Britain and the United States arising out of the Clayton and Bulwer treaty of April, 1850, have been finally adjusted. . . .

In my last annual message I stated that overtures had been made by the British government for this purpose (to settle the Central American questions) in a friendly spirit, which I cordially reciprocated. Their proposal was to withdraw these questions from direct negotiation between the two governments, but to accomplish the same object by a negotiation between the British government and each of the Central American Republics whose territorial interests are immediately involved. The settlement was to be made in accordance with the general tenor of the interpretation placed upon the Clayton and Bulwer treaty by the United States, with certain modifications. As negotiations are still pending upon this basis, it would not be proper for me now to communicate their present condition. A final settlement of these questions is greatly to be desired, as this would wipe out the last remaining subject of dispute between the two countries.

Our relations with the great empires of France and Russia, as well as with all other governments on the continent of Europe, except that of Spain, continue to be of the most friendly character. . . .

It has been made known to the world by my predecessors that the United States have on several occasions endeavored to acquire Cuba from Spain by honorable negotiation. If this were accomplished, the last relic of the African slave trade would instantly disappear. We would not, if we could, acquire Cuba in any other manner. This is due to our national character. All the territory which we have acquired since the origin of the Government has been by fair purchase from France, Spain, and Mexico or by the free and voluntary act of the independent State of Texas in blending her destinies with our own. This course we shall ever pursue, unless circumstances should occur which we do not now anticipate, rendering a departure from it clearly justifiable under the imperative and overruling law of self-preservation.

The island of Cuba, from its geographical position, commands the mouth of the Mississippi and the immense and annually increasing trade, foreign and coastwise, from the valley of that noble river, now embracing half the sovereign States of the Union. With that island under the dominion of a distant foreign power this trade, of vital importance to these States, is exposed to the danger of being destroyed in time of war, and it has hitherto been subjected to perpetual injury and annoyance in time of peace. Our relations with Spain, which ought to be of the most friendly character, must always be placed in jeopardy whilst the existing colonial government over the island shall remain in its present condition.

Whilst the possession of the island would be of vast importance to the United States, its value to Spain is comparatively unimportant. Such was the relative situation of the parties when the great Napoleon transferred Louisiana to the United States. Jealous as he ever was of the national honor and interests of France, no person throughout the world has imputed blame to him for accepting a pecuniary equivalent for this cession.

The publicity which has been given to our former negotiations upon this subject and the large appropriation which may be required to effect the purpose render it expedient before making another attempt to renew the negotiation that I should lay the whole subject before Congress. This is especially necessary, as it may become indispendable to success that I should be intrusted with the means of making an advance to the Spanish government immediately after the signing of the treaty, without awaiting the ratification of it by the Senate. I am encouraged to make this suggestion by the example of Mr. Jefferson previous to the purchase of Louisiana from France and by that of Mr. Polk in view of the acquisition of territory from Mexico. I refer the whole subject to Congress and commend it to their careful consideration. . . .

The political condition of the narrow isthmus of Central America, through which transit routes pass between the Atlantic and Pacific oceans, present a subject of deep interest to all commercial nations. It is over these transits that a large proportion of the trade and travel between the European and Asiatic continents is destined to pass. To the United States these routes are of incalculable importance as a means of communication between their Atlantic and Pacific possessions. . . .

A treaty was signed on the 16th day of November, 1857, by the Secretary of State and minister of Nicaragua, under the stipulations of which the use and protection of the transit route would have been secured not only to the United States, but equally to all other nations. How and on what pretext this treaty has failed to receive the ratification of the Nicaraguan Government will appear by the papers herewith communicated from the State Department. The principal objection seems to have been to the provision authorizing the United States to employ force to keep the route open in case Nicaragua should fail to perform her duty in this respect. From the feebleness of that Republic, its frequent changes of government, and its constant internal dissensions, this had become a most important stipulation, and one essentially necessary, not only for the security of the route, but for the safety of American citizens passing and repassing to and from our Pacific possessions. Were such a stipulation embraced in a treaty between the United States and Nicaragua, the knowledge of this fact would of itself most probably prevent hostile parties from committing aggressions on the route, and render our actual interference for its protection unnecessary.

The Executive of this country in its intercourse with foreign nations is limited to the employment of diplomacy alone. When this fails it can proceed no further. It cannot legitimately resort to force without the direct authority of Congress, except in resisting and repelling hostile attacks. It would have no authority to enter the territories of Nicaragua even to prevent the destruction of the transit and protect the lives and property of our own citizens on their passage. It is true that on a sudden emergency of this character the President would direct any armed force in the vicinity to march to their relief, but in doing this he would act upon his own responsibility.

Under these circumstances I earnestly recommend to Congress the passage of an act authorizing the President, under such restrictions as they may deem proper, to employ the land and naval forces of the United States in preventing the transit from being obstructed or closed by lawless violence, and in protecting the lives and property of American citizens travelling thereupon, requiring at the same time that these forces shall be withdrawn the moment the danger shall have passed away. Without such a provision our citizens will be constantly exposed to interruption in their progress and to lawless violence.

A similar necessity exists for the passage of such an act for the protection of the Panama and Tehuantepec routes. . . .

When Congress met in December last the business of the country had just been crushed by one of those periodical revulsions which are the inevitable consequence of our unsound and extravagant system of bank credits and inflated currency. With all the elements of national wealth in abundance, our manufactures were suspended, our useful public and private enterprises were arrested, and thousands of laborers were deprived of employment and reduced to want. Universal distress prevailed among the commercial, manufacturing, and mechanical classes. This revulsion was felt the more severely in the United States because similar causes had produced the like deplorable effects throughout the commercial nations of Europe. All were experiencing sad reverses at the same moment. . . .

No government, and especially a government of such limited powers as that of the United States, could have prevented the late revulsion. The whole commercial world seemed for years to have been rushing to this catastrophe. The same ruinous consequences would have followed in the

United States whether the duties upon foreign imports had remained as they were under the tariff of 1846 or had been raised to a much higher standard. The tariff of 1857 had no agency in the result. The general causes existing throughout the world could not have been controlled by the legislation of any particular country.

The periodical revulsions which have existed in our past history, must continue to return at intervals so long as our present unbounded system of bank credit shall prevail. . . . But this subject was treated so much at large in my last annual message that I shall not now pursue it further. Still, I respectfully renew the recommendation in favor of the passage of a uniform bankrupt law applicable to banking institutions. This is all the direct power over the subject which I believe the Federal Government possesses. Such a law would mitigate, though it might not prevent, the evil. The instinct of self-preservation might produce a wholesome restraint upon their banking business if they knew in advance that a suspension of specie payments would inevitably produce their civil death. . . .

I would again call your attention to the construction of a Pacific railroad. Time and reflection have but served to confirm me in the truth and justice of the observations which I made on this subject in my last annual message, to which I beg leave respectfully to refer.

It is freely admitted that it would be inexpedient for this Government to exercise the power of constructing the Pacific railroad by its own immediate agents. Such a policy would increase the patronage of the Executive to a dangerous extent, and introduce a system of jobbing and corruption which no vigilance on the part of Federal officials could either prevent or detect. This can only be done by the keen eye and active and careful supervision of individual and private interest. . . .

I cannot conclude without performing the agreeable duty of expressing my gratification that Congress so kindly responded to the recommendation of my last annual message by affording me sufficient time before the close of their late session for the examination of all the bills presented to me for approval. This change in the practice of Congress has proved to be a wholesome reform. It exerted a beneficial influence on the transaction of legislative business and elicited the general approbation of the country. It enabled Congress to adjourn with that dignity and deliberation so becoming to the representatives of this great Republic, without having crowded into general appropriation bills provisions foreign to their nature and doubtful constitutionality and expediency. Let me warmly and strongly commend this precedent established by themselves as a guide to their proceedings during the present session.

JAMES BUCHANAN.

MESSAGE ON THE CONSTITUTION OF KANSAS
February 2, 1858

*In the face of demands that all Kansas be allowed
an honest election to vote on the Lecompton Constitution, Buchanan nevertheless decided that the vote
on the slavery proposition was a valid vote on the
constitution itself. Under the circumstances, he presented the constitution to Congress as the document
on which admission of Kansas as a state should be
determined. His own appointee, Governor Robert J.
Walker, resigned; Senator Stephen A. Douglas fought
the entry of Kansas on these terms, but the bill accepting the Lecompton Constitution won in the Senate.
The House, however, favoring "honest popular sovereignty," defeated the measure.*

To the Senate and House of Representatives of the United States:
. . .It has been solemnly adjudged by the highest judicial tribunal
known to our laws that slavery exists in Kansas by virtue of the Constitution of the United States. Kansas is therefore at this moment as much a
slave State as Georgia or South Carolina. Without this equality of the
sovereign States composing the Union would be violated and the use and
enjoyment of a Territory acquired by the common treasure of all the
States would be closed against the people and the property of nearly half
the members of the Confederacy. Slavery can therefore never be prohibited
in Kansas except by means of a constitutional provision, and in no other
manner can this be obtained so promptly, if a majority of the people
desire it, as by admitting it into the Union under its present constitution.
On the other hand, should Congress reject the constitution under the
idea of affording the disaffected in Kansas a third opportunity of prohibiting slavery in the State, which they might have done twice before if in
the majority, no man can foretell the consequences.
If Congress, for the sake of those men who refused to vote for dele-

gates to the convention when they might have excluded slavery from the constitution, and who afterwards refused to vote on the 21st December last, when they might, as they claim, have stricken slavery from the constitution, should now reject the State because slavery remains in the constitution, it is manifest that the agitation upon this dangerous subject will be renewed in a more alarming form than it has ever yet assumed.

Every patriot in the country had indulged the hope that the Kansas and Nebraska act would put a final end to the slavery agitation, at least in Congress, which had for more than twenty years convulsed the country and endangered the Union. This act involved great and fundamental principles, and if fairly carried into effect will settle the question. Should the agitation be again revived, should the people of the sister States be again estranged from each other with more than their former bitterness, this will arise from a cause, so far as the interests of Kansas are concerned, more trifling and insignificant than has ever stirred the elements of a great people into commotion. To the people of Kansas the only practical difference between admission or rejection depends simply upon the fact whether they can themselves more speedily change the present constitution to be submitted to Congress hereafter. Even if this were a question of mere expediency, and not of right, the small difference of time one way or the other is of not the least importance when contrasted with the evils which must necessarily result to the whole country from a revival of the slavery agitation.

In considering this question it should never be forgotten that in proportion to its insignificance, let the decision be what it may so far as it may affect the few thousand inhabitants of Kansas who have from the beginning resisted the constitution and the laws, for this very reason the rejection of the constitution will be so much the more keenly felt by the people of fourteen of the States of this Union, where slavery is recognized under the Constitution of the United States.

Again the speedy admission of Kansas into the Union would restore peace and quiet to the whole country. Already the affairs of this Territory have engrossed an undue proportion of public attention. They have sadly affected the friendly relations of the people of the States with each other and alarmed the fears of patriots for the safety of the Union. Kansas once admitted into the Union, the excitement becomes localized and will soon die away for want of outside ailment. Then every difficulty will be settled at the ballot box.

Besides—and this is no trifling consideration—I shall then be enabled to withdraw the troops of the United States from Kansas and employ them on branches of service where they are much needed. They have been kept there, on the earnest importunity of Governor Walker, to maintain the existence of the Territorial government and secure the execution of the laws. He considered that at least 2,000 regular troops, under the command of General Harney, were necessary for this purpose. Acting upon his reliable information, I have been obliged in some degree to interfere with the expedition to Utah in order to keep down rebellion in Kansas. This has involved a very heavy expense to the Government. Kansas once admitted, it is believed there will no longer be any occasion there for troops of the United States.

I have thus performed my duty on this important question, under a deep sense of responsibility to God and my country. My public life will terminate within a brief period, and I have no other object of earthly ambition than to leave my country in a peaceful and prosperous condition and to live in the affections and respect of my countrymen. The dark and ominous clouds which now appear to be impending over the Union I conscientiously believe may be dissipated with honor to every portion of it by the admission of Kansas during the present session of Congress, whereas if she should be rejected I greatly fear these clouds will become darker and more ominous than any which have ever yet threatened the Constitution and the Union.

JAMES BUCHANAN.

THIRD ANNUAL MESSAGE
December 19, 1859

> *More than any previous document, this message points up how Buchanan weakened the presidential office. He placed squarely on the shoulders of Congress the responsibility for solving the problems which confronted the country. Among other things, he stated that "without the authority of Congress" the president could not fire a gun except to repel attacks of an enemy, therefore he could do nothing about Southern cessation threats; that by failing to pass deficiency bills Congress arrested the action of government and threatened its continued existence. Once again Buchanan reflected his great interest in the acquisition of Cuba by proposing its purchase. This was one of the most important elements in his Latin America policy. The proposal never reached the floor of Congress.*

Fellow-Citizens of the Senate and House of Representatives:

. . .Whilst it is the duty of the President "from time to time, to give to Congress information of the state of the Union," I shall not refer in detail to the recent sad and bloody occurrences at Harper's Ferry. Still, it is proper to observe that these events, however bad and cruel in themselves, derive their chief importance from the apprehension that they are but symptoms of an incurable disease in the public mind, which may break out in still more dangerous outrages and terminate at last in an open war by the North to abolish slavery in the South.

Whilst for myself I entertain no such apprehension, they ought to afford a solemn warning to us all to beware of the approach of danger. Our Union is a stake of such inestimable value as to demand our constant and watchful vigilance for its preservation. In this view, let me implore my countrymen, North and South, to cultivate the ancient feelings of mutual forbearance and good will toward each other and strive to allay the demon spirit of sectional hatred and strife now alive in the land. This advice proceeds from the heart of an old public functionary whose service commenced in the last generation, among the wise and conservative statesmen of that day, now nearly all passed away, and whose first and dearest earthly wish is to leave his country tranquil, prosperous, united, and powerful. . . .

I cordially congratulate you upon the final settlement by the Supreme Court of the United States of the question of slavery in the Territories, which had presented an aspect so truly formidable at the commencement of my Administration. The right has been established of every citizen to take his property of any kind, including slaves, into the common Territories belonging equally to all the States of the Confederacy, and to have it protected there under the Federal Constitution. Neither Congress nor a Territorial legislature nor any human power has any authority to annul or impair this vested right. The supreme judicial tribunal of the country which is a coordinate branch of the Government, has sanctioned and affirmed these principles of constitutional law, so manifestly just in themselves and so well calculated to promote peace and harmony among the States. It is a striking proof of the sense of justice which is inherent in our people that the property in slaves has never been disturbed, to my knowledge, in any of the Territories. Even throughout the late troubles in Kansas there has not been any attempt, as I am credibly informed, to interfere in a single instance with the right of the master. Had any such attempt been made, the judiciary would doubtless have afforded an adequate remedy. Should they fail to do this hereafter, it will then be time enough to strengthen their hands by further legislation. Had it been decided that either Congress or the territorial legislature possess the power to annul or impair the right to property in slaves, the evil would be intolerable. . . .

All lawful means at my command have been employed, and shall continue to be employed, to execute the laws against the African slave trade. After a most careful and rigorous examination of our coasts and a thorough investigation of the subject, we have not been able to discover that any slaves have been imported into the United States except the cargo by the *Wanderer*, numbering between three and four hundred. Those engaged in this unlawful enterprise have been rigorously prosecuted, but not with as much success as their crimes have deserved. A number of them are still under prosecution. . . .

But we are obliged as a Christian and moral nation to consider what would be the effect upon unhappy Africa itself if we should reopen the slave trade. This would give the trade an impulse and extension which it has never had even in its palmiest days. The numerous victims required to supply it would convert the whole slave coast into a perfect pandemonium, for which this country would be held responsible in the eyes

both of God and man. Its petty tribes would then be constantly engaged
in predatory wars against each other for the purpose of seizing slaves
to supply the American market. All hopes of African civilization would
thus be ended.

On the other hand, when a market for African slaves shall no longer
be furnished in Cuba, and thus all the world be closed against this
trade, we may then indulge a reasonable hope for the gradual improvement of Africa. The chief motive of war among the tribes will cease
whenever there is no longer any demand for slaves. The resources of
that fertile but miserable country might then be developed by the hand
of industry and afford subjects for legitimate foreign and domestic commerce. In this manner Christianity and civilization may gradually penetrate
the existing gloom.

The wisdom of the course pursued by this Government towards China
has been vindicated by the event. Whilst we sustained a neutral position
in the war waged by Great Britain and France against the Chinese Empire, our late minister, in obedience to his instructions, judiciously co-
operated with the ministers of these powers in all peaceful measures to
secure by treaty the just concessions demanded by the interests of foreign
commerce. The result is, that satisfactory treaties have been concluded
with China by the respective ministers of the United States, Great Britain,
France, and Russia. . . .

It affords me much satisfaction to inform you that all our difficulties
with the Republic of Paraguay have been satisfactorily adjusted. It happily
did not become necessary to employ the force for this purpose which
Congress had placed at my command under the joint resolution of 2d
June, 1858. On the contrary, the President of that Republic, in a friendly
spirit, acceded promptly to the just and reasonable demands of the Government of the United States. Our commissioner arrived at Assumption,
the capital of the Republic, on the 25th of January, 1859, and left it on
the 17th of February, having in three weeks ably and successfully accomplished all the objects of his mission. The treaties which he concluded
will be immediately submitted to the Senate.

In the view that the employment of other than peaceful means might
become necessary to obtain "just satisfaction" from Paraguay, a strong
naval force was concentrated in the waters of the La Plata to await con-
tingencies whilst our Commissioner ascended the rivers to Assumption.
The Navy Department is entitled to great credit for the promptness,
efficiency, and economy with which this expedition was fitted out and
conducted. It consisted of 19 armed vessels, great and small, carrying
200 guns and 2,500 men, all under the command of the veteran and
gallant Shubrick. The entire expenses of the expedition have been de-
frayed out of the ordinary appropriations for the naval service, except

the sum of $289,000, applied to the purchase of seven of the steamers constituting a part of it, under the authority of the naval appropriation act of the 3d March last. It is believed that these steamers are worth more than their cost, and they are all now usefully and actively employed in the naval service.

The appearance of so large a force, fitted out in such a prompt manner, in the far distant waters of the La Plata, and the admirable conduct of the officers and men employed in it, have had a happy effect in favor of our country throughout all that remote portion of the world.

Our relations with the great empires of France and Russia, as well as with all other governments on the continent of Europe, unless we may except that of Spain, happily continue to be of the most friendly character.

In my last annual message I presented a statement of the unsatisfactory condition of our relations with Spain, and I regret to say that this has not materially improved.

Without special reference to other claims, even the "Cuban claims," the payment of which has been ably urged by our ministers and in which more than a hundred of our citizens are directly interested, remain unsatisfied, notwithstanding both their justice and their amount ($128,635.54) had been recognized and ascertained by the Spanish government itself. . . .

I need not repeat the arguments which I urged in my last annual message in favor of the acquisition of Cuba by fair purchase. My opinions on the measure remain unchanged. I therefore again invite the serious attention of Congress to this important subject. Without a recognition of this policy on their part it will be almost impossible to institute negotiations with any reasonable prospect of success.

Until a recent period there was good reason to believe that I should be able to announce to you on the present occasion that our difficulties with Great Britain arising out of the Clayton and Bulwer treaty, had been finally adjusted in a manner alike honorable and satisfactory to both parties. From causes, however, which the British government had not anticipated, they have not yet completed treaty arrangements with the Republics of Honduras and Nicaragua, in pursuance of the understanding between the two Governments. It is, nevertheless, confidently expected that this good work will ere long be accomplished. . . .

I regret to inform you that there has been no improvement in the affairs of Mexico since my last annual message, and I am again obliged to ask the earnest attention of Congress to the unhappy condition of that Republic. . . .

I repeat the recommendation contained in my last annual message, that authority may be given to the President to establish one or more temporary military posts across the Mexican line in Sonora and Chihuahua, where these may be necessary to protect the lives and property of American and Mexican citizens against the incursions and depredations of the Indians, as well as of lawless rovers on that remote region. . . . The population of Arizona, now numbering more than 10,000 souls, are practically destitute of government, of laws, or of any regular administration of justice. Murder, rape, and other crimes are committed with impunity. I therefore again call the attention of Congress to the necessity for establishing a Territorial government over Arizona.

The treaty with Nicaragua of the 16th of February, 1857, to which I referred in my last annual message, failed to receive the ratification of the Government of that Republic, for reasons which I need not enumerate. A similar treaty has been since concluded between the parties, bearing date on the 16th March, 1859, which has been already ratified by the Nicaraguan Congress. This will be immediately submitted to the Senate for their ratification. Its provisions cannot, I think, fail to be acceptable to the people of both countries.

Our claims against the Governments of Costa Rica and Nicaragua remain unredressed, though they are pressed in an earnest manner and not without hope of success.

I deem it to be my duty once more earnestly to recommend to Congress the passage of a law authorizing the President to employ the naval force at his command for the purpose of protecting the lives and property of American citizens passing in transit across the Panama, Nicaragua, and Tehuantepec routes, against sudden and lawless outbreaks and depredations. . . .

I would also recommend to Congress that authority be given to the President to employ the naval force to protect American merchant vessels, their crews, and cargoes, against violent and lawless seizure and confiscation in the ports of Mexico and the Spanish American States when these countries may be in a disturbed and revolutionary condition. The mere knowledge that such an authority had been conferred, as I have already stated, would of itself in a great degree prevent the evil. Neither would this require any additional appropriation for the naval service.

The chief objection urged against the grant of this authority is that Congress by conferring it would violate the Constitution, that it would be a transfer of the war-making, or, strictly speaking, the war-declaring, power to the Executive. If this were well founded, it would, of course, be conclusive. A very brief examination, however, will place this objection at rest. . . .

It will not be denied that the general "power to declare war" is without limitation and embraces within itself not only what writers on the law of nations term a public or perfect war, but also an imperfect war, and, in short, every species of hostility however confined or limited. Without the authority of Congress the President cannot fire a hostile gun in any case except to repel the attacks of an enemy. It will not be doubted that under this power Congress could, if they thought proper, authorize the President to employ the force at his command to seize a vessel belonging to an American citizen which had been illegally and unjustly captured in a foreign port and restore it to its owner. But can Congress only act after the fact, after the mischief has been done? Have they no power to confer upon the President the authority in advance to furnish instant redress should such a case afterward occur? Must they wait until the mischief has been done, and can they apply the remedy only when it is too late? To confer this authority to meet future cases under circumstances strictly specified is as clearly within the war-declaring power as such an authority conferred upon the President by act of Congress after the deed had been done. In the progress of a great nation many exigencies must arise imperatively requiring that Congress should authorize the President to act promptly on certain conditions which may or may not afterward arise. Our history has already presented a number of such cases. . . .

I would again express a most decided opinion in favor of the construction of a Pacific railroad, for the reasons stated in my two last annual messages. When I reflect upon what would be the defenseless condition of our States and Territories west of the Rocky Mountains in case of a war with a naval power sufficiently strong to interrupt all intercourse with them by the route across the Isthmus, I am still more convinced then ever of the vast importance of this railroad. I have never doubted the constitutional competency of Congress to provide for its construction, but this exclusively under the war-making power. . . .

We have yet scarcely recovered from the habits of extravagant expenditure produced by our overflowing Treasury during several years prior to the commencement of my Administration. The financial reverses which we have since experienced ought to teach us all to scrutinize our expenditures with the greatest vigilance, and to reduce them to the lowest possible point. . . .

In conclusion I would again commend to the just liberality of Congress the local interests of the District of Columbia. Surely the city bearing the name of Washington, and destined, I trust, for ages to be the capital of our united, free, and prosperous Confederacy, has strong claims on our favorable regard.

JAMES BUCHANAN.

VETO OF THE HOMESTEAD BILL
June 22, 1860

*Buchanan's veto of the Homestead Bill has often been
cited as the act which elected Lincoln. The veto message itself never mentioned the real reasons for the
veto which was in fact Buchanan's fear that it would
encourage a frenzied migration into the new West;
this was the mistake of the Kansas-Nebraska Bill and
he was determined not to repeat it. The Republicans,
on the other hand, were motivated by a desire to win
favor in the North and among antislavery people in
general. Indeed, they anticipated a veto since Buchanan
had earlier made known his opposition to giving away
the public domain in this manner. Nevertheless, the
veto probably did help to elect Lincoln as it certainly
hurt Douglas and the Democrats who lost favor with
free workingmen and free farmers, a combination which
had been the base of northern Democrats.*

To the Senate of the United States:

I return with my objections to the Senate, in which it originated, the
bill entitled "An act to secure homesteads to actual settlers on the public
domain, and for other purposes," presented to me on the 20th instant.

This bill gives to every citizen of the United States "who is the head of
a family," and to every person of foreign birth residing in the country
who has declared his intention to become a citizen, though he may not
be the head of a family, the privilege of appropriating to himself 160
acres of Government land, of settling and residing upon it for five years;
and should his residence continue until the end of this period, he shall
then receive a patent on the payment of 25 cents per acre, or one-fifth
of the present Government price. During this period, the land is protected from all the debts of the settler.

This bill also contains a cession to the States of all the public lands
within their respective limits "which have been subject to sale at private
entry, and which remain unsold after the lapse of thirty years." This
provision embraces a present donation to the States of 12,229,731

acres, and will, from time to time, transfer to them large bodies of such lands which, from peculiar circumstances, may not be absorbed by private purchase and settlement.

To the actual settler this bill does not make an absolute donation, but the price is so small that it can scarcely be called a sale. It is nominally 25 cents per acre; but considering this is not to be paid until the end of five years, it is in fact reduced to about 18 cents per acre, or one-seventh of the present minimum price of the public lands. In regard to the States, it is an absolute and unqualified gift.

1. This state of facts raises the question whether Congress, under the Constitution, has the power to give away the public lands either to States or individuals. On this question I expressed a decided opinion in my message to the House of Representatives of the 24th February, 1859, returning the agricultural college bill. This opinion remains unchanged. The argument then used applies as a constitutional objection with greater force to the present bill. *There* it had the plea of consideration, growing out of a specific beneficial purpose; *here* it is an absolute gratuity to the States, without the pretext of consideration. I am compelled for want of time in these the last hours of the session to quote largely from this message.

I presume the general proposition will be admitted that Congress does not possess the power to make donations of money already in the Treasury, raised by taxes on the people, either to States or individuals.

But it is contended that the public lands are placed upon a different footing from money raised by taxation and that the proceeds arising from their sale are not subject to the limitations of the Constitution, but may be appropriated or given away by Congress, at its own discretion, to States, corporations, or individuals, for any purpose they may deem expedient.

The advocates of this bill attempt to sustain their position upon the language of the second clause of the third section of the fourth article of the Constitution, which declares that "the Congress shall have power to dispose and make all needful rules and regulations respecting the territory or other property belonging to the United States." They contend that by a fair interpretation of the words "dispose of" in this clause Congress possesses the power to make this gift of public lands to the States for purposes of education.

It would require clear and strong evidence to induce the belief that the framers of the Constitution, after having limited the powers of Congress to certain, precise, and specific objects, intended by employing the words "dispose of," to give that body unlimited power over the vast public domain. It would be a strange anomaly indeed to have created two funds—the one by taxation, confined to the execution of the enumerated powers delegated to Congress, and the other from the public lands, applicable to all subjects, foreign and domestic, which Congress might designate. That this fund should be "disposed of," not to pay the debts of the United States, nor "to raise and support armies," nor "to provide and maintain a navy," nor to accomplish any one of the other great objects enumerated in the Constitution, but be diverted from them to pay the debts of the States, to educate their people, and to carry into effect any other measure of their domestic policy. This would be to confer upon Congress a vast and irresponsible authority utterly at war with the well-known jealousy of Federal power which prevailed at the formation of the Constitution. The natural intendment would be that as the Constitution confined Congress to well-defined specific powers, the funds placed at their command, whether in land or money, should be appropriated to the performance of the duties corresponding with these powers. If not, a Government has been created with all its other powers carefully limited, but without any limitation in respect to the public lands.

But I cannot so read the words "dispose of" as to make them embrace the idea of "giving away." The true meaning of words is always to be ascertained by the subject to which they are applied and the known general intent of the law-giver. Congress is a trustee under the Constitution for the people of the United States to "dispose of" their public lands; and I think I may venture to assert with confidence that no case can be found in which a trustee in the position of Congress has been authorized to *"dispose of"* property by its owner where it has ever been held that these words authorized such trustee to give away the funds intrusted to his care. No trustee, when called upon to account for the disposition of the property placed under his management before any judicial tribunal, would venture to present such a plea in his defense. . . .

2. It will prove unequal and unjust in its operation among the actual settlers themselves.

The first settlers of a new country are a most meritorious class. They brave the dangers of savage warfare, suffer the privations of a frontier life, and with the hand of toil bring the wilderness into cultivation. The "old settlers," as they are everywhere called, are public benefactors. This class have all paid for their lands at the Government price, or $1.25 per acre. They have constructed roads, established schools, and laid the foundation of prosperous commonwealths. Is it just, is it equal that after they have accomplished all this by their labor new settlers should come in among them and receive their farms at the price of 25 or 18 cents per acre? Surely the old settlers, as a class, are entitled to at least equal benefits with the new. If you give the new settlers their land for a comparatively nominal price, upon every principle of equality and justice you will be obliged to refund out of the common treasury the difference which the old have paid above the new settlers for their land.

3. This bill will do great injustice to the old soldiers who have received land warrants for their services in fighting the battles of their country. It will greatly reduce the market value of these warrants. Already their value has sunk for 160 acre warrants, to 67 cents per acre, under an apprehension that such a measure as this might become a law. What price would they command when any head of a family may take possession of a quarter section of land and not pay for it until the end of five years, and then at the rate of only 25 cents per acre? The magnitude of the interest to be affected will appear in the fact that there are outstanding unsatisfied land warrants reaching back to the last war with Great Britain, and even Revolutionary times, amounting, in round numbers, to seven and a half million of acres.

4. This bill will prove unequal and unjust in its operation, because, from its nature it is confined to one class of our people. It is a boon exclusively conferred upon the cultivators of the soil. Whilst it cheerfully is admitted that these are the most numerous and useful class of our fellow-citizens and eminently deserve all the advantages which our laws have already extended to them, yet there should be no new legislation which would operate to the injury or embarrassment of the large body of respectable artisans and laborers. The mechanic who emigrates to the West and pursues his calling must labor long before he can purchase a quarter section of land whilst the tiller of the soil who accompanies him obtains a farm at once by the bounty of the Government. The numerous body of mechanics in our large cities cannot, even by emigrating to the West, take advantage of the provisions of this bill without entering upon a new occupation, for which their habits of life have rendered them unfit.

5. This bill is unjust to the old States of the Union in many respects; and amongst these States so far as the public lands are concerned we may enumerate every State east of the Mississippi with the exception of Wisconsin and a portion of Minnesota.

It is a common belief within our limits that the older States of the Confederacy do not derive their proportionate benefit from the public lands. This is not a just opinion. It is doubtful whether they could be rendered more beneficial to these States under any other system than that which at present exists. Their proceeds go into the common Treasury to accomplish the objects of the Government, and in this manner all the States are benefited in just proportion. But to give this common inheritance away would deprive the old States of their just proportion of this revenue without holding out any the least corresponding advantage. Whilst it is our common glory that the new States have become so prosperous and populous, there is no good reason why the old States should offer premiums to their own citizens to emigrate from them to the West. That land of promise presents in itself sufficient allurements to our young and enterprising citizens without any advantageous aid. The offer of free farms would probably have a powerful effect in encouraging emigration, especially from States like Illinois, Tennessee and Kentucky, to the west of the Mississippi, and could not fail to reduce the price of property within their limits. An individual in States thus situated would not pay its fair value for land when by crossing the Mississippi he could go upon the public lands and obtain a farm almost without money and without price.

6.   This bill will open one vast field for speculation. Men will not pay $1.25 for lands when they can purchase them for one-fifth of that price. Large numbers of actual settlers will be carried out by capitalists upon agreements to give them half of the land for the improvement of the other half. This cannot be avoided. Secret arrangements of this kind will be numerous. In the entry of graduated lands the experience of the Land Office justifies this objection.

7.   We ought ever to maintain the most perfect equality between native and naturalized citizens. They are equal, and ought always to remain equal before the laws. Our laws welcome foreigners to our shores and their rights will ever be respected. Whilst these are the sentiments on which I have acted through life, it is not, in my opinion, expedient to proclaim to all the nations of the earth that whoever shall arrive in this country from a foreign shore and declare his intention to become a citizen shall receive a farm of 160 acres at a cost of 25 or 20 cents per acre if he will only reside on it and cultivate it. The invitation extends to all, and if this bill becomes a law we may have numerous actual settlers from China and other Eastern nations enjoying its benefits on the great Pacific slope. The bill makes a distinction in favor of such persons over native and naturalized citizens. When applied to such citizens, it is confined to such as are the heads of families but when applicable to persons of foreign birth recently arrived on our shores there is no such restriction. Such persons need not be the heads of families provided they have filed a declaration of intention to become citizens. Perhaps this distinction was an inadvertence, but it is nevertheless, a part of the bill.

8.   The bill creates an unjust distinction between persons claiming the benefit of the pre-emption laws. Whilst it reduces the price of the land to existing pre-emptors to 62-1/2 cents per acre and gives them a credit on this sum for two years from the present date, no matter how long they may have hitherto enjoyed the land, future pre-emptors will be compelled to pay double this price per acre. There is no reason or justice in this discrimination.

9. The effect of this bill on the public revenue must be apparent to all. Should it become a law, the reduction of the price of land to actual settlers to 25 cents per acre, with a credit of five years, and the reduction of its price to existing pre-emptors to 62-1/2 cents per acre, with a credit of two years, will so diminish the sale of other public lands as to render the expectation of future revenue from that source, beyond the expenses of survey and management, illusory. The Secretary of the Interior estimated the revenue from the public lands for the next fiscal year at $4,000,000, on the presumption that the present land system would remain unchanged. Should this bill become a law, he does not believe that $1,000,000 will be derived from this source.

10. This bill lays the axe at the root of our present admirable land system. The public land is an inheritance of vast value to us and to our descendants. It is a resource to which we can resort in the hour of difficulty and danger. It has been managed heretofore with the greatest wisdom under existing laws. In this management the rights of actual settlers have been conciliated with the interests of the Government. The price to all has been reduced from $2 per acre to $1.25 for fresh lands, and the claims of actual settlers have been secured by our pre-emption laws. Any man can now acquire a title in fee simple to a homestead of eighty acres, at the minimum price of $1.25 per acre for $100. Should the present system remain, we shall derive a revenue from the public lands of $10,000,000 per annum, when the bounty-land warrants are satisfied, without oppression to any human being. In time of war, when all other sources of revenue are seriously impaired, this will remain intact. It may become the best security for public loans hereafter, in times of difficulty and danger, as it has been heretofore. Why should we impair or destroy the system at the present moment? What necessity exists for it?

The people of the United States have advanced with steady but rapid strides to their condition of power and prosperity. They have been guided in their progress by the fixed principle of protecting the equal rights of all, whether they be rich or poor. No agrarian sentiment has ever prevailed among them. The honest poor man, by frugality and industry can, in any part of our country, acquire a competence for himself and his family, and in doing this he feels that he eats the bread of independence. He desires no charity, either from the Government or from his neighbors. This bill, which proposes to give him land at an almost nominal price out of the property of the Government, will go far to demoralize the people and repress this noble spirit of independence. It may introduce among us those pernicious social theories which have proved so disastrous in other countries.

JAMES BUCHANAN

DEFENSE OF PRESIDENTIAL RIGHTS AND POWERS
June 22, 1860

Buchanan had been charged with using corrupt influence to validate the Lecompton Constitution and on March 5, 1860, John Covode was made head of a committee of the House of Representatives to investigate the charges. The President sent a message of protest on March 28, and again on June 22. In this latter message Buchanan attempts to show that on grounds of constitutionality and of principle he had been unfairly maligned and outlines his view of the proper role of the president.

WASHINGTON, *June 22, 1860.*

To the House of Representatives:

In my message to the House of Representatives of the 28th March last I solemnly protested against the creation of a committee, at the head of which was placed my accuser, for the purpose of investigating whether the President had, "by money, patronage, or other improper means, sought to influence the action of Congress or any committee thereof for or against the passage of any law appertaining to the rights of any State or Territory." I protested against this because it was destitute of any specification; because it referred to no particular act to enable the President to prepare for his defense; because it deprived him of the constitutional guards which, in common with every citizen of the United States, he possesses for his protection, and because it assailed his constitutional independence as a coordinate branch of the Government.

There is an enlightened justice, as well as a beautiful symmetry, in every part of the Constitution. This is conspicuously manifested in regard to impeachments. The House of Representatives possesses "the sole power of impeachment," the Senate "the sole power to try all impeachments;" and the impeachable offenses are "treason, bribery, or other high crimes or misdemeanors." The practice of the House from the earliest times had been in accordance with its own dignity, the rights of the accused, and the demands of justice. At the commencement of each judicial investigation which might lead to an impeachment specific charges were always preferred; the accused had an opportunity of cross-examining the witnesses, and he was placed in full possession of the precise nature of the offense which he had to meet. An impartial and elevated standing committee was charged with this investigation, upon which no member inspired with the ancient sense of honor and justice would have served had he ever expressed an opinion against the accused. Until the present occasion it was never deemed proper to transform the accuser into the judge and to confer upon him the selection of his own committee.

The charges made against me in vague and general terms were of such a false and atrocious character that I did not entertain a moment's apprehension for the result. They were abhorrent to every principle instilled into me from my youth and every practice of my life, and I did not believe it possible that the man existed who would so basely perjure himself as to swear to the truth of any such accusations. In this conviction I am informed I have not been mistaken.

In my former protest, therefore, I truly and emphatically declared that it was made for no reason personal to myself, but because the proceedings of the House were in violation of the rights of the coordinate executive branch of the Government, subversive of its constitutional independence, and if unresisted would establish a precedent dangerous and embarrassing to all my successors. Notwithstanding all this, if the committee had not transcended the authority conferred upon it by the resolution of the House of Representatives, broad and general as this was, I should have remained silent upon the subject. What I now charge is that they have acted as though they possessed unlimited power, and without any warrant whatever in the resolution under which they were appointed, have pursued a course not merely at war with the constitutional rights of the Executive, but tending to degrade the Presidential office itself to such a degree as to render it unworthy of the acceptance of any man of honor or principle.

The resolution of the House, so far as it is accusatory of the President, is confined to an inquiry whether he had used corrupt or improper means to influence the action of Congress or any of its committees on legislative measures pending before them—nothing more, nothing less. I have not learned through the newspapers or in any other mode that the committee have touched the other accusatory branch of the resolution, charging the President with a violation of duty in failing to execute some law or laws. This branch of the resolution is therefore out of the question. By what authority, then, have the committee undertaken to investigate the course of the President in regard to the convention which framed the Lecompton constitution? By what authority have they undertaken to pry into our foreign relations for the purpose of assailing him on account of the instructions given by the Secretary of State to our minister in Mexico relative to the Tehuantepec route? By what authority have they inquired into the causes of removal from office, and this from the parties themselves removed, with a view to prejudice his character, notwithstanding this power of removal belongs exclusively to the President under the Constitution, was so decided by the First Congress in the year 1789, and has accordingly ever since been exercised? There is in the resolution no pretext of authority for the committee to investigate the question of the printing of the post-office blanks; nor is it to be supposed that the House, if asked, would have granted such an authority, because this question had been previously committed to two other committees—one in the Senate and the other in the House. Notwithstanding this absolute want of power, the committee rushed into this investigation in advance of all other subjects.

The committee proceeded for months, from March 22, 1860, to examine *ex parte* and without any notice to myself into every subject which could possibly affect my character. Interested and vindictive witnesses were summoned and examined before them; and the first and only information of their testimony which, in almost every instance, I received was obtained from the publication of such portions of it as could injuriously affect myself in the New York journals. It mattered not that these statements were, so far as I have learned, disproved by the most respectable witnesses who happened to be on the spot. The telegraph was silent respecting these contradictions. It was a secret committee in regard to the testimony in my defense, but it was public in regard to all the testimony which could by possibility reflect on my character. The poison was left to produce its effect upon the public mind, whilst the antidote was carefully withheld.

In their examinations the committee violated the most sacred and honorable confidences existing among men. Private correspondence, which a truly honorable man would never even entertain a distant thought of divulging, was dragged to light. Different persons in official and confidential relations with myself, and with whom it was supposed I might have held conversations the revelation of which would do me injury, were examined. Even members of the Senate and members of my own Cabinet, both my constitutional advisers, were called upon to testify, for the purpose of discovering something, if possible, to my discredit.

The distribution of the patronage of the Government is by far the most diagreeable duty of the President. Applicants are so numerous and their applications are pressed with such eagerness by their friends, both in and out of Congress, that the selection of one for any desirable office gives offense to many. Disappointed applicants, removed officers, and those who for any cause, real or imaginary, had become hostile to the Administration presented themselves or were invited by a summons to appear before the committee. These are the most dangerous witnesses. Even with the best intentions they are so influenced by prejudice and disappointment that they almost inevitably discolor truth. They swear to their own version of private conversations with the President without the possibility of contradiction. His lips are sealed, and he is left at their mercy. He can not, as a coordinate branch of the Government, appear before a committee of investigation to contradict the oaths of such witnesses. Every coward knows that he can employ insulting language against the President with impunity, and every false or prejudiced witness can attempt to swear away his character before such a committee without the fear of contradiction.

Thus for months, whilst doing my best at one end of the Avenue to perform my high and responsible duties to the country, has there been a committee of the House of Representatives in session at the other end of the Avenue spreading a drag net, without the shadow of authority from the House, over the whole Union, to catch any disappointed man willing to malign my character; and all this in secret conclave. The lion's mouth at Venice, into which secret denunciations were dropped, is an apt illustration of the Covode committee. The star-chamber, tyrannical and odious as it was, never proceeded in such a manner. For centuries there has been nothing like it in any civilized country, except the revolutionary tribunal of France in the days of Robespierre. Now I undertake to state and to prove that should the proceedings of the committee be sanctioned by the House and become a precedent for future times the balance of the Constitution will be entirely upset, and there will no longer remain the three coordinate and independent branches of the Government--legislative, executive, and judicial. The worst fears of the patriots and statesmen who framed the Constitution in regard to the usurpations of the legislative on the executive and judicial branches will then be realized. In the language of Mr. Madison, speaking on this very subject in the forty-eighth number of the Federalist:

"In a representative republic, where the executive magistracy is carefully limited, both in the extent and duration of its power, and where the legislative power is exercised by an assembly which is inspired, by a supposed influence over the people, with an intrepid confidence in its own strength, which is sufficiently numerous to feel all the passions which actuate a multitude, yet not so numerous as to be incapable of pursuing the objects of its passions by means which reason prescribes, it is against the enterprising ambition of this department that the people ought to indulge all their jealousy and exhaust all their precautions.''

And in the expressive and pointed language of Mr. Jefferson, when speaking of the tendency of the legislative branch of Government to usurp the rights of the weaker branches:

'' The concentrating these in the same hands is precisely the definition of despotic government. It will be no alleviation that these powers will be exercised by a plurality of hands, and not by a single one. One hundred and seventy-three despots would surely be as oppressive as one. Let those who doubt it turn their eyes on the Republic of Venice. As little will it avail us that they are chosen by ourselves. An elective despotism was not the government we fought for, but one which should not only be founded on free principles, but in which the powers of government should be so divided and balanced among several bodies of magistracy as that no one could transcend their legal limits without being effectually checked and controlled by the others.''

Should the proceedings of the Covode committee become a precedent, both the letter and spirit of the Constitution will be violated. One of the three massive columns on which the whole superstructure rests will be broken down. Instead of the Executive being a coordinate it will become a subordinate branch of the Government. The Presidential office will be dragged into the dust. The House of Representatives will then have rendered the Executive almost necessarily subservient to its wishes, instead of being independent. How is it possible that two powers in the State can be coordinate and independent of each other if the one claims and exercises the power to reprove and to censure all the official acts and all the private conversations of the other, and this upon *ex parte* testimony before a secret inquisitorial committee—in short, to assume a general censorship over the other? The idea is as absurd in public as it would be in private life. Should the President attempt to assert and maintain his own independence, future Covode committees may dragoon him into submission by collecting the hosts of disappointed office hunters, removed officers, and those who desire to live upon the public Treasury, which must follow in the wake of every Administration, and they in secret conclave will swear away his reputation. Under such circumstances he must be a very bold man should he not surrender at discretion and consent to exercise his authority according to the will of those invested with this terrific power. The sovereign people of the several States have elected him to the highest and most honorable office in the world. He is their only direct representative in the Government. By their Constitution they have made him Commander in Chief of their Army and Navy. He represents them in their intercourse with foreign nations. Clothed with their dignity and authority, he occupies a proud position before all nations, civilized and savage. With the consent of the Senate, he appoints all the important officers of the Government. He exercises the veto power, and to that extent controls the legislation of Congress. For the performance of these high duties he is responsible to the people of the several States, and not in any degree to the House or Representatives.

Shall he surrender these high powers, conferred upon him as the representative of the American people for their benefit, to the House to be exercised under their overshadowing influence and control? Shall he alone of all the citizens of the United States be denied a fair trial? Shall he alone not be "informed of the nature and cause of the accusation" against him? Shall he alone not "be confronted with the witnesses" against him? Shall the House of Representatives, usurping the powers of the Senate, proceed to try the President through the agency of a secret committee of the body, where it is impossible he can make any defense, and then, without affording him an opportunity of being heard, pronounce a judgment of censure against him? The very same rule might be applied for the very same reason to every judge of every court of the United States. From what part of the Constitution is this terrible secret inquisitorial power derived? No such express power exists. From which of the enumerated powers can it be inferred? It is true the House can not pronounce the formal judgment against him of "removal from office," but they can by their judgment of censure asperse his reputation and thus to the extent of their influence render the office contemptible. An example is at hand of the reckless manner in which this power of censure can be employed in high party times. The House on a recent occasion have attempted to degrade the President by adopting the resolution of Mr. John Sherman declaring that he, in conjunction with the Secretary of Navy, "by receiving and considering the party relations of bidders for contracts and the effect of awarding contracts upon pending elections, have set an example dangerous to the public safety and deserving the reproof of this House."

It will scarcely be credited that the sole pretext for this vote of censure was the simple fact that in disposing of the numerous letters of every imaginable character which I daily receive I had in the usual course of business referred a letter from Colonel Patterson, of Philadelphia, in relation to a contract, to the attention of the Secretary of the Navy, the head of the appropriate Department, without expressing or intimating any opinion whatever on the subject; and to make the matter if possible still plainer, the Secretary had informed the committee that *the President did not in any manner interfere in this case, nor has he in any other*

case of contract since I have been in the Department." The absence of
all proof to substain this attempt to degrade the President, whilst it mani-
fests the venom of the shaft aimed at him, has destroyed the vigor of
the bow.

To return after this digression: Should the House, by the institution
of Covode committees, votes of censure, and other devices to harass the
President, reduce him to subservience to their will and render him their
creature, then the well-balanced Government which our fathers framed
will be annihilated. This conflict has already been commenced in earnest
by the House against the Executive. A bad precedent rarely, if ever, dies.
It will, I fear, be pursued in the time of my successors, no matter what
may be their political character. Should secret committees be appointed
with unlimited authority to range over all the words and actions, and, if
possible, the very thoughts, of the President with a view to discover
something in his past life prejudicial to his character from parasites and
informers, this would be an ordeal which scarcely any mere man since
the fall could endure. It would be to subject him to a reign of terror
from which the stoutest and purest heart might shrink. I have passed
triumphantly through this ordeal. My vindication is complete. The committee have reported no resolution looking to an impeachment against
me; no resolution of censure; not even a resolution pointing out any
abuses in any of the Executive Departments of the Government to be cor-
rected by legislation. This is the highest commendation which could be bestowed on the heads of these Departments. The sovereign people of the
States will, however, I trust, save my successors, whoever they may be, from
any such ordeal. They are frank, bold, and honest. They detest delators
and informers. I therefore, in the name and as the representative of this
great people, and standing upon the ramparts of the Constitution which
they "have ordained and established," do solemnly protest against these
unprecedented and unconstitutional proceedings.

There was still another committee raised by the House on the 6th
March last, on motion of Mr. Hoard, to which I had not the slightest
objection. The resolution creating it was confined to specific charges,
which I have ever since been ready and willing to meet. I have at all
times invited and defied fair investigation upon constitutional principles.
I have received no notice that this committee have ever proceeded to the
investigation.

Why should the House of Representatives desire to encroach on the
other departments of the Government? Their rightful powers are ample
for every legitimate purpose. They are the impeaching body. In their
legislative capacity it is their most wise and wholesome perogative to
institute rigid examinations into the manner in which all departments of
the Government are conducted, with a view to reform abuses, to promote

economy, and to improve every branch of administration. Should they find reason to believe in the course of their examinations that any grave offense had been committed by the President or any officer of the Government rendering it proper, in their judgment, to resort to impeachment, their course would be plain. They would then transfer the question from their legislative to their accusatory jurisdiction, and take care that in all the preliminary judicial proceedings preparatory to the vote of articles of impeachment the accused should enjoy the benefit of cross-examining the witnesses and all the other safeguards with which the Constitution surrounds every American citizen.

If in a legislative investigation it should appear that the public interest required the removal of any officer of the Government, no President has ever existed who, after giving him a fair hearing, would hesitate to apply the remedy.

This I take to be the ancient and well-established practice. An adherence to it will best promote the harmony and the dignity of the intercourse between the coordinate branches of the Government and render us all more respectable both in the eyes of our own countrymen and of foreign nations.

JAMES BUCHANAN

FOURTH ANNUAL MESSAGE
December 3, 1860

In this (last annual) message, Buchanan denied the right of secession and also stated his conviction that if a state should adopt such an unconstitutional measure the Federal Government had no power, under the Constitution, to compel her to stay in the Union. But he went on to say that state ordinances of secession could not absolve its people from obeying the laws of the United States. He proposed an "explanatory amendment" of the Constitution which would secure slaveholders in their constitutional rights.

Fellow-Citizens of the Senate and House of Representatives:

Throughout the year since our last meeting the country has been eminently prosperous in all its material interests. The general health has been excellent, our harvests have been abundant, and plenty smiles throughout the land. Our commerce and manufactures have been prosecuted with energy and industry, and have yielded fair and ample returns. In short, no nation in the tide of time has ever presented a spectacle of greater material prosperity than we have done until within a very recent period.

Why is it, then, that discontent now so extensively prevails, and the Union of the States, which is the source of all these blessings, is threatened with destruction?

The long-continued and intemperate interference of the Northern people with the question of slavery in the Southern States has at length produced its natural effects. The different sections of the Union are now arrayed against each other, and the time has arrived, so much dreaded by the Father of his Country, when hostile geographical parties have been formed.

I have long foreseen and often forewarned my countrymen of the now impending danger. This does not proceed solely from the claim on the part of Congress or the Territorial legislatures to exclude slavery from the Territories, nor from the efforts of different States to defeat the execution of the fugitive-slave law. All or any of these evils might have been endured by the South without danger to the Union (as others have been) in the hope that time and reflection might apply the remedy. The immediate peril arises not so much from these causes as from the fact that the incessant and violent agitation of the slavery question throughout the North for the last quarter of a century has at length produced its malign influence on the slaves and inspired them with vague notions of freedom. Hence a sense of security no longer exists around the family altar. This feeling of peace at home has given place to apprehensions of servile insurrections. Many a matron throughout the South retires at night in dread of what may befall herself and children before the morning. Should this apprehension of domestic danger, whether real or imaginary, extend and intensify itself until it shall pervade the masses of the Southern people, then disunion will become inevitable. Self-preservation is the first law of nature, and has been implanted in the heart of man by his Creator for the wisest purpose; and no political union, however fraught with blessings and benefits in all other respects, can long continue if the necessary consequence be to render the homes and firesides of nearly half the parties to it habitually and hopelessly insecure. Sooner or later the bonds of such a union must be severed. It is my conviction that this fatal period has not yet arrived, and my prayer to God is that He would preserve the Constitution and the Union throughout all generations.

But let us take warning in time and remove the cause of danger. It can not be denied that for five and twenty years the agitation at the North against slavery has been incessant. In 1835 pictorial handbills and inflammatory appeals were circulated extensively throughout the South of a character to excite the passion of the slaves, and, in the language of General Jackson, "to stimulate them to insurrection and produce all the horrors of a servile war." This agitation has ever since been continued by the public press, by the proceedings of State and county conventions and by abolition sermons and lectures. The time of Congress has been occupied in violent speeches on this never-ending subject, and appeals, in pamphlet and other forms, indorsed by distinguished names, have been sent forth from this central point and spread broadcast over the Union.

How easy would it be for the American people to settle the slavery question forever and to restore peace and harmony to this distracted country! They, and they alone, can do it. All that is necessary to accomplish the object, and all for which the slave States have ever contended, is to be let alone and permitted to manage their domestic institutions in their own way. As sovereign States, they, and they alone, are responsible before God and the world for the slavery existing among them. For this the people of the North are not more responsible and have no more right to interfere than with similar institutions in Russia or in Brazil.

Upon their good sense and patriotic forbearance I confess I still greatly rely. Without their aid it is beyond the power of any President, no matter what may be his own political proclivities, to restore peace and harmony among the States. Wisely limited and restrained as is his power under our Constitution and laws, he alone can accomplish but little for good or for evil on such a momentus question.

And this brings me to observe that the election of any of our fellow-citizens to the office of President does not of itself afford just cause for dissolving the Union. This is more especially true if his election has been effected by a mere plurality, and not a majority of the people, and has resulted from transient and temporary causes, which may probably never again occur. In order to justify a resort to revolutionary resistance, the Federal Government must be guilty of "a deliberate, palpable, and dangerous exercise" of powers not granted by the Constitution. The late Presidential election, however, has been held in strict conformity with its express provisions. How, then, can the result justify a revolution to destroy this very Constitution? Reason, justice, a regard for the Constitution, all require that we shall wait for some overt and dangerous act on the part of the President elect before resorting to such a remedy. It is said, however, that the antecedents of the President elect have been sufficient to justify the fears of the South that he will attempt to invade their constitutional rights. But are such apprehensions of contingent danger in the future sufficient to justify the immediate destruction of the noblest system of government ever devised by mortals? From the very nature of his office and its high responsibilities he must necessarily be conservative. The stern duty of administering the vast and complicated concerns of this Government affords in itself a guaranty that he will not attempt any violation of a clear constitutional right.

After all, he is no more than the chief executive officer of the Government. His province is not to make but to execute the laws. And it is a remarkable fact in our history that, notwithstanding the repeated efforts of the antislavery party, no single act has ever passed Congress, unless we may possibly except the Missouri compromise, impairing in the slightest degree the rights of the South to their property in slaves; and it may also be observed, judging from present indications, that no probability exists of the passage of such an act by a majority of both Houses, either in the present or the next Congress. Surely under these circumstances we ought to be restrained from present action by the precept of Him who spake as man never spoke, that "sufficient unto the day is the evil thereof." The day of evil may never come unless we shall rashly bring it upon ourselves.

It is alleged as one cause for immediate secession that the Southern States are denied equal rights with the other States in the common Territories. But by what authority are these denied? Not by Congress, which has never passed, and I believe never will pass, any act to exclude slavery from these Territories; and certainly not by the Supreme Court, which has solemnly decided that slaves are property, and, like all other property, their owners have a right to take them into the common Territories and hold them under the protection of the Constitution.

So far, then, as Congress is concerned, the objection is not to anything they have already done, but to what they may do hereafter. It will surely be admitted that this apprehension of future danger is no good reason for an immediate dissolution of the Union. . . .

Only three days after my inauguaration the Supreme Court of the United States solemnly adjudged that this power did not exist in a Territorial legislature. Yet such has been the factious temper of the times that the correctness of this decision has been extensively impugned before the people, and the question has given rise to angry political conflicts throughout the country. Those who have appealed from this judgment of our highest constitutional tribunal to popular assemblies would, if they could, invest a Territorial legislature with power to annul the sacred rights of property. This power Congress is expressly forbidden by the Federal Constitution to exercise. Every State legislature in the Union is forbidden by its own constitution to exercise it. It can not be exercised in any State except by the people in their highest sovereign capacity, when framing or amending their State constitution. In like manner it can only be exercised by the people of a Territory represented in a convention of delegates for the purpose of framing a constitution preparatory to admission as a State into the Union. Then, and not until then, are they invested with power to decide the question whether slavery shall or shall not exist within their limits. This is an act of sovereign authority, and not of subordinate Territorial legislation. Were it otherwise, then indeed would the equality of the States in the Territories be destroyed, and the rights of property in slaves would depend not upon the guaranties of the Constitution, but upon the shifting majorities of an irresponsible Territorial legislature. Such a doctrine, from its intrinsic unsoundness, can not long influence any considerable portion of our people, much less can it afford a good reason for a dissolution of the Union.

The most palpable violations of constitutional duty which have yet been committed consist in the acts of different State legislatures to defeat the execution of the fugitive-slave law. It ought to be remembered, however, that for these acts neither Congress nor any President can justly be held responsible. Having been passed in violation of the Federal Constitution, they are therefore null and void. All the courts, both State and national, before whom the question has arisen have from the beginning declared the fugitive-slave law to be constitutional. . . . Here, then, a clear case is presented in which it will be the duty of the next President, as it has been my own, to act with vigor in executing this supreme law against the conflicting enactments of State legislatures. Should he fail in the performance of this high duty, he will then have manifested a disregard of the Constitution and laws, to the great injury of the people of nearly one-half of the States of the Union. But are we to presume in advance that he will thus violate his duty? This would be at war with every principle of justice and Christian charity. Let us wait for the overt act. The fugitive-slave law has been carried into execution in every contested case since the commencement of of the present Administration, though often, it is to be regretted, with great loss and inconvenience to the master and with considerable expense to the Government. Let us trust that the State legislatures will repeal their unconstitutional and obnoxious enactments. Unless this shall be done without unnecessary delay, it is impossible for any human power to save the Union.

The Southern States, standing on the basis of the Constitution, have a right to demand this act of justice from the States of the North. Should it be refused, then the Constitution, to which all the States are parties, will have been willfully violated by one portion of them in a provision essential to the domestic security and happiness of the remainder. In that event the injured States, after having first used all peaceful and constitutional means to obtain redress, would be justified in revolutionary resistance to the Government of the Union.

I have purposely confined my remarks to revolutionary resistance, because it has been claimed within the last few years that any State, whenever this shall be its sovereign will and pleasure, may secede from the Union in accordance with the Constitution and without any violation of the constitutional rights of the other members of the Confederacy; that as each became parties to the Union by the vote of its own people assembled in convention, so any one of them may retire from the Union in a similar manner by the vote of such a convention.

In order to justify secession as a constitutional remedy, it must be on the principle that the Federal Government is a mere voluntary association of States, to be dissolved at pleasure by any one of the contracting parties. If this be so, the Confederacy is a rope of sand, to be penetrated and dissolved by the first adverse wave of public opinion in any of the States. In this manner our thirty-three States may resolve themselves into as many petty, jarring, and hostile republics, each one retiring from the Union without responsibility whenever any sudden excitement might impel them to such a course. By this process a Union might be entirely broken into fragments in a few weeks which cost our forefathers many years of toil, privation, and blood to establish.

Such a principle is wholly inconsistent with the history as well as the character of the Federal Constitution. After it was framed with the greatest deliberation and care it was submitted to conventions of the people of the several States for ratification. Its provisions were discussed at length in these bodies, composed of the first men of the country. Its opponents contended that it conferred powers upon the Federal Government dangerous to the rights of the States, whilst its advocates maintained that under a fair construction of the instrument there was no foundation for such apprehensions. In that mighty struggle between the first intellects of this or any other country it never occurred to any individual, either among its opponents or advocates, to assert or even to intimate that their efforts were all vain labor, because the moment that any State felt herself aggrieved she might secede from the Union. What a crushing argument would this have proved against those who dreaded that the rights of the States would be endangered by the Constitution! . . .

It was intended to be perpetual, and not be annulled at the pleasure of any one of the contracting parties. The old Articles of Confederation were entitled "Articles of Confederation and Perpetual Union between the States," and by the thirteenth article it is expressly declared that "the articles of the Confederation shall be inviolably observed by every State, and the Union shall be perpetual." The preamble to the Constitution of the United States, having express reference to the Articles of Confederation, recites that it was established "in order to form a more perfect union." And yet it is contended that this "more perfect union" does not include the essential attribute of perpetuity.

But that the Union was designed to be perpetual appears conclusively from the nature and extent of the powers conferred by the Constitution on the Federal Government. These powers embrace the very highest attributes of national sovereignty. They place both the sword and the purse under its control. Congress has power to make war and to make peace, to raise and support armies and navies, and to conclude treaties with foreign governments. It is invested with the power to coin money and to regulate the value thereof, and to regulate commerce with foreign nations and among the several States. It is not necessary to enumerate the other high powers which have been conferred upon the Federal Government. In order to carry the enumerated powers into effect, Congress possesses the exclusive right to lay and collect duties on imports, and, in common with the States, to lay and collect all other taxes. . . .

In order to carry into effect these powers, the Constitution has established a perfect Government in all its forms—legislative, executive, and judicial; and this Government to the extent of its powers acts directly upon the individual citizens of every State, and executes its own decrees by the agency of its own officers. In this respect it differs entirely from the Government under the old Confederation, which was confined to making requisitions on the States in their sovereign character. This left it in the discretion of each whether to obey or to refuse, and they often declined to comply with such requisitions. It thus became necessary for the purpose of removing this barrier and "in order to form a more perfect union" to establish a Government which could act directly upon the people and execute its own laws without the intermediate agency of the States. This has been accomplished by the Constitution of the United States. In short, the Government created by the Constitution, and deriving its authority from the sovereign people of each of the several States, has precisely the same right to exercise its power over the people of all these States in the enumerated cases that each one of them possesses over subjects not delegated to the United States, but "reserved to the States respectively or to the people."

To the extent of the delegated powers the Constitution of the United States is as much a part of the constitution of each State and is as binding upon its people as though it had been textually inserted therein.

This Government, therefore, is a great and powerful Government, invested with all the attributes of sovereignty over the special subjects to which its authority extends. Its framers never intended to implant in its bosom the seeds of its own destruction, nor were they at its creation guilty of the absurdity of providing for its own dissolution. It was not intended by its framers to be the baseless fabric of a vision, which at the touch of the enchanter would vanish into thin air, but a substantial and mighty fabric, capable of resisting the slow decay of time and of defying the storms of ages. Indeed, well may the jealous patriots of that day have indulged fears that a Government of such high powers might violate the reserved rights of the States, and wisely did they adopt the rule of a strict construction of these powers to prevent the danger. But they did not fear, nor had they any reason to imagine, that the Constitution would ever be so interpreted as to enable any State by her own act, and without the consent of her sister States, to discharge her people from all or any of their federal obligations.

It may be asked, then, Are the people of the States without redress against the tyranny and oppression of the Federal Government? By no means. The right of resistance on the part of the governed against the oppression of their governments cannot be denied. It exists independently of all constitutions, and has been exercised at all periods of the world's history. Under it old governments have been destroyed and new ones have taken their place. It is embodied in strong and express language in our own Declaration of Independence. But the distinction must ever be observed that this is revolution against an established government, and not a voluntary secession from it by virtue of an inherent constitutional right. In short, let us look the danger fairly in the face. Secession is neither more nor less than revolution. It may or it may not be a justifiable revolution, but still it is revolution.

What, in the meantime, is the responsibility and true position of the Executive? He is bound by solemn oath, before God and the country, "to take care that the laws be faithfully executed," and from this obligation he can not be absolved by any human power. But what if the performance of this duty, in whole or in part, has been rendered impracticable by events over which he could have exercised no control? Such at the present moment is the case throughout the State of South Carolina so far as the laws of the United States to secure the administration of justice by means of the Federal judiciary are concerned. All the Federal officers within its limits through whose agency alone these laws can be carried into execution have already resigned. We no longer have a district judge, a district attorney, or a marshall in South Carolina. In fact, the whole machinery of the Federal Government necessary for the distribution of remedial justice among the people has been demolished, and it would be difficult, if not impossible, to replace it. . . .

Apart from the execution of the laws, so far as they may be practicable, the Executive has no authority to decide what shall be the relations between the Federal Government and South Carolina. He has been invested with no such discretion. He possesses no power to change the relations heretofore existing between them, much less to acknowledge the independence of that State. This would be to invest a mere executive officer with the power of recognizing the dissolution of the confederacy among our thirty-three sovereign States. It bears no resemblance to the recognition of a foreign *de facto* government, involving no such responsibility. Any attempt to do this would, on his part, be a naked act of usurpation. It is therefore my duty to submit to Congress the whole question in all its bearings. The course of events is so rapidly hastening forward that the emergency may soon arise when you may be called upon to decide the momentous question whether you possess the power by force of arms to compel a State to remain in the Union. I should feel myself recreant to my duty were I not to express an opinion on this important subject.

The question fairly stated is, Has the Constitution delegated to Congress the power to coerce a State into submission which is attempting to withdraw or has actually withdrawn from the Confederacy? If answered in the affirmative, it must be on the principle that the power has been conferred upon Congress to declare and to make war against a State. After much serious reflection I have arrived at the conclusion that no such power has been delegated to Congress or to any other department of the Federal Government. It is manifest upon an inspection of the Constitution that this is not among the specific and enumerated powers granted to Congress, and it is equally apparent that its exercise is not "necessary and proper for carrying into execution" any one of these powers. So far from this power having been delegated to Congress, it was expressly refused by the Convention which framed the Constitution. . . .

Without descending to particulars, it may be safely asserted that the power to make war against a State is at variance with the whole spirit and intent of the Constitution. Suppose such a war should result in the conquest of a State; how are we to govern it afterwards? Shall we hold it as a province and govern it by despotic power? In the nature of things, we could not by physical force control the will of the people and compel them to elect Senators and Representatives to Congress and to perform all the other duties depending upon their own volition and required from the free citizens of a free State as a constituent member of the Confederacy.

But if we possessed this power, would it be wise to exercise it under existing circumstances? The object would doubtless be to preserve the Union. War would not only present the most effectual means of destroying it, but would vanish all hope of its peaceable reconstruction. Besides, in the fraternal conflict a vast amount of blood and treasure would be expended, rendering future reconciliation between the States impossible. In the meantime, who can foretell what would be the sufferings and privations of the people during its existence?

The fact is that our Union rests upon public opinion, and can never be cemented by the blood of its citizens shed in civil war. If it can not live in the affections of the people, it must one day perish. Congress possesses many means of preserving it by conciliation, but the sword was not placed in their hand to preserve it by force.

But may I solemnly be permitted to invoke my countrymen to pause and deliberate before they determine to destroy this the grandest temple which has ever been dedicated to human freedom since the world began? It has been consecrated by the blood of our fathers, by the glories of the past, and by the hopes of the future. The Union has already made us the most prosperous, and ere long will, if preserved, render us the most powerful, nation on the face of the earth. In every foreign region of the globe the title of American citizen is held in the highest respect, and when pronounced in a foreign land it causes the hearts of our countrymen to swell with honest pride. Surely when we reach the brink of the yawning abyss we shall recoil with horror from the last fatal plunge.

By such a dread catastrophe the hopes of the friends of freedom throughout the world would be destroyed, and a long night of leaden despotism would enshroud the nations. Our example for more than eighty years would not only be lost, but it would be quoted as a conclusive proof that man is unfit for self-government.

It is not every wrong—nay, it is not every grevious wrong—which can justify a resort to such a fearful alternative. This ought to be the last desperate remedy of a despairing people, after every other constitutional means of conciliation had been exhausted. We should reflect that under this free Government there is an incessant ebb and flow in public opinion. The slavery question, like everything human, will have its day. I firmly believe that it has reached and passed the culminating point. But if in the midst of the existing excitement the Union shall perish, the evil may then become irreparable.

Congress can contribute much to avert it by proposing and recommending to the legislatures of the several States the remedy for existing evils which the Constitution has itself provided for its own preservation. This has been tried at different critical periods of our history, and always with eminent success. It is to be found in the fifth article, providing for its own amendment. . . .

This is the very course which I earnestly recommend in order to obtain an "explanatory amendment" of the Constitution on the subject of slavery. This might originate with the Congress or the State legislatures, as may be deemed most advisable to attain the object. The explanatory amendment might be confined to the final settlement of the true construction of the Constitution on three special points:

1. An express recognition of the right of property in slaves in the States where it now exists or may herafter exist.

2. The duty of protecting this right in all the common Territories throughout their Territorial existence, and until they shall be admitted as States into the Union, with or without slavery, as their constitutions may prescribe.

3. A like recognition of the right of the master to have his slave who has escaped from one State to another restored and "delivered up" to him, and of the validity of the fugitive-slave law enacted for this purpose, together with a declaration that all State laws impairing or defeating this right are violations of the Constitution, and are consequently null

and void. It may be objected that this construction of the Constitution has already been settled by the Supreme Court of the United States, and what more ought to be required? The answer is that a very large proportion of the people of the United States still contest the correctness of this decision, and never will cease from agitation and admit its binding force until clearly established by the people of the several States in their sovereign character. Such an explanatory amendment would, it is believed, forever terminate the existing dissensions, and restore peace and harmony among the States.

It ought not to be doubted that such an appeal to the arbitrament established by the Constitution itself would be received with favor by all the States of the Confederacy. In any event, it ought to be tried in a spirit of conciliation before any of these States shall separate themselves from the Union. . . .

JAMES BUCHANAN

SPECIAL MESSAGE ON SOUTH CAROLINA'S SECESSION
January 8, 1861

Buchanan sent a special message concerning relations with South Carolina in which he makes clear that only Congress had the responsibility and the power to make war or to legislate the removal of grievances. For his part, he would take no risks of starting war or "even to furnish an excuse for it by an act of this government." Under the circumstances, he was refraining from sending reinforcements to Major Anderson in Charleston Harbor rather than risk furnishing a provocation or even a pretext for a further provacative act on the part of South Carolina.

To the Senate and the House of Representatives:

At the opening of your present session, I called your attention to the dangers which threatened the existence of the Union. I expressed my opinion freely concerning the original causes of those dangers, and recommended such measures as I believed would have the effect of tranquilizing the country and saving it from the peril in which it had been needlessly and most unfortunately involved. Those opinions and recommendations I do not propose now to repeat. My own convictions upon the whole subject remain unchanged.

The fact that a great calamity was impending over the nation was even at that time acknowledged by every intelligent citizen. It had already made itself felt throughout the length and breadth of the land. The necessary consequence of the alarm thus produced were most deplorable. The imports fell off with a rapidity never known before except in time of war, in the history of our foreign commerce; the Treasury was unexpectedly left without the means which it had reasonably counted upon to meet the public engagements; trade was paralyzed; manufactures were stopped; the best public securities suddenly sunk in the market; every species of property depreciated more or less, and thousands of poor men who depended upon their daily labor for their daily bread were turned out of employment.

I deeply regret that I am not able to give you any information upon the state of the Union which is more satisfactory than what I was then obliged to communicate. On the contrary, matters are still worse at present than they were. When Congress met, a strong hope pervaded the whole public mind that some amicable adjustment of the subject would speedily be made by the representatives of the States and of the people which might restore peace between the conflicting sections of the country. That hope has been diminished by every hour of delay, and as the prospect of a bloodless settlement fades away the public distress becomes more and more aggravated. As evidence of this it is only necessary to say that the Treasury notes authorized by the act of 17th of December last were advertised according to the law and that no responsible bidder offered to take any considerable sum at par at a lower rate of interest than 12 per cent. From these facts it appears that in a government organized like ours domestic strife, or even a well-grounded fear of civil hostilities, is more destructive to our public and private interests than the most formidable foreign war.

In my annual message I expressed the conviction, which I have long deliberately held, and which recent reflection has only tended to deepen and confirm, that no State has a right by its own to secede from the Union or throw off its federal obligations at pleasure. I also declared my opinion to be that even if that right existed and should be exercised by any State of the Confederacy the executive department of this Government had no authority under the Constitution to recognize its validity by acknowledging the independence of such State. This left me no alternative, as the chief executive officer under the Constitution of the United States, but to collect the public revenues and to protect the public property so far as this might be practicable under existing laws. This is still my purpose. My province is to execute and not to make the laws. It belongs to Congress exclusively to repeal, to modify, or to enlarge their provisions to meet exigencies as they may occur. I possess no dispensing power.

I certainly had no right to make aggressive war upon any State, and I am perfectly satisfied that the Constitution has wisely withheld that power even from Congress. But the right and the duty to use military force defensively against those who resist the federal officers in the execution of their legal functions and against those who assail the property of the Federal Government is clear and undeniable.

But the dangerous and hostile attitude of the States towards each other has already far transcended and cast in the shade the ordinary executive duties already provided for by law, and has assumed such vast and alarming proportions as to place the subject entirely above and beyond Executive control. The fact cannot be disguised that we are in the midst of a great revolution. In all its various bearings, therefore, I commend the question to Congress as the only human tribunal under Providence possessing the power to meet the existing emergency. To them exclusively belongs the power to declare war or to authorize the employment of military force in all cases contemplated by the Constitution, and they alone possess the power to remove grievances which might lead to war and to secure peace and union to this distracted country. On them, and on them alone, rests the responsibility.

The Union is a sacred trust left by our Revolutionary fathers to their descendants, and never did any other people inherit so rich a legacy. It has rendered us prosperous in peace and triumphant in war. The national flag has floated in glory over every sea. Under its shadow American citizens have found protection and respect in all lands beneath the sun. . . .

The greatest aggravation of the evil, and that which would place us in the most unfavorable light both before the world and posterity, is, as I am firmly convinced, that the secession movement has been chiefly based upon a misapprehension at the South of the sentiments of the majority in several of the Northern States. Let the question be transferred from political assemblies to the ballot-box, and the people themselves would speedily redress the serious grievances which the South have suffered. But, in Heaven's name, let the trial be made before we plunge into armed conflict upon the mere assumption that there is no other alternative. Time is a great conservative power. Let us pause at this momentous point and afford the people, both North and South, an opportunity for reflection. Would that South Carolina had been convinced of this truth before her precipitate action! I therefore appeal through you to the people of the country to declare in their might that the Union must and shall be preserved by all constitutional means. I most earnestly recommend that you devote yourselves exclusively to the question how this can be accomplished in peace. All other questions, when compared to this, sink into insignificance. The present is no time for palliations. Action, prompt action, is required. A delay in Congress to prescribe or to recommend a distinct and practical proposition for conciliation may drive us to a point from which it will be almost impossible to recede.

A common ground on which conciliation and harmony can be produced is surely not unattainable. The proposition to compromise by letting the North have exclusive control of the territory above a certain line and to give Southern institutions protection below that line ought to receive universal approbation. In itself, indeed, it may not be entirely satisfactory, but when the alternative is between a reasonable concession on both sides and a destruction of the Union it is an imputation upon the patriotism of Congress to assert that its members will hesitate for a moment.

Even now the danger is upon us. In several of the States which have not yet seceded the forts, arsenals, and magazines of the United States have been seized. This is by far the most serious step which has been taken since the commencement of the troubles. This public property has long been left without garrisons and troops for its protection, because no person doubted its security under the flag of the country in any State of the Union. Besides, our small Army has scarcely been sufficient to guard our remote frontiers against Indian incursions. The seizure of this property from all appearances, has been purely aggressive, and not in resistance to any attempt to coerce a State or States to remain in the Union.

At the beginning of these unhappy troubles I determined that no act of mine should increase the excitement in either section of the country. If the political conflict were to end in a civil war, it was my determined purpose not to commence it nor even to furnish an excuse for it by any act of this Government. My opinion remains unchanged that justice as well as sound policy requires us still to seek a peaceful solution of the questions at issue between the North and the South. Entertaining this conviction, I refrained even from sending reinforcements to Major Anderson, who commanded the forts in Charleston Harbor, until an absolute necessity for doing so should make itself apparent, lest it might unjustly be regarded as a meanace of military coercion, and thus furnish, if not a provocation, at least a pretext for an outbreak on the part of South Carolina. No necessity for these reinforcements seemed to exist. I was assured by distinguished and upright gentlemen of South Carolina that no attack upon Major Anderson was intended, but that, on the contrary, it was the desire of the State authorities as much as it was my own to avoid the fatal consequences which must eventually follow a military collision. . . .

In conclusion it may be permitted to me to remark that I have often warned my countrymen of the dangers which now surround us. This may be the last time I shall refer to the subject officially. I feel that my duty has been faithfully, though it may be imperfectly, performed, and, whatever the result may be, I shall carry to my grave the consciousness that I at least meant well for my country.

JAMES BUCHANAN

BIBLIOGRAPHICAL AIDS

The emphasis in this and subsequent volumes in the **Presidential Chronologies** series will be on the administrations of the presidents. The more important works on other aspects of their lives, either before or after their terms in office, are included since they may contribute to an understanding of the presidential careers.

The following bibliography is critically selected. Many additional titles may be found in the works cited and in the standard guide. The student might also wish to consult **Reader's Guide to Periodical Literature** and **Social Sciences and Humanities Index** (formerly **International Index**) for recent articles in scholarly journals.

Additional chronological information not included in this volume because it did not relate directly to the president may be found in the **Encyclopedia of American History,** edited by Richard B. Morris, revised edition (New York, 1965).

Asterisks after titles refer to books currently available in paperback editions.

SOURCE MATERIALS

The amount of source material dealing with James Buchanan is greatly limited, and what there is is largely confined to the manuscript collections in the Lancaster County Historical Society Library. A number of specialized items are held in the Library of Dickinson College and the Library of Franklin and Marshall College. Beyond this, the Manuscripts Division, Library of Congress, holds much of the material dealing with Buchanan's presidential administration.

John Basset Moore's (ed.) **The Works of James Buchanan,** 12 vols. (Phila., 1906) contains Buchanan's printed correspondence and a substantial part of his official messages and memoranda. This publication is a limited one (7,650 copies) and is available in a number of the larger public and university libraries.

BIOGRAPHIES

Curtis, George T. **The Life of James Buchanan.** 2 vols. New York, 1883. This is an "authorized" biography by an eminent historian of the period. It contains a considerable amount of source material in the form of personal correspondence. While the bias and judgments of the biographer show throughout, the study has considerable value because of the access Curtis had to Buchanan's family and friends as well as to personal papers.

Klein, Philip S. **President James Buchanan.** University Park, Pa. 1962. A work of impressive scholarship as well as a readable one. Like the younger Schlesinger, Klein offers the reader detailed and comprehensive notes and bibliography, yet the study is not weighed down by the extensive scholarship. This will probably remain the definitive biography of Buchanan for a long time to come.

MONOGRAPHS AND ESSAYS ON BUCHANAN

Auchampaugh, Philip C. **James Buchanan and His Cabinet on the Eve of Secession.** Boston, 1926.* A more favorable interpretation of Buchanan's role than is customary.

Fish, Carl Russell. "James Buchanan." **Dictionary of American Biography,** III, 207-214. New York, 1929.

Klingberg, Frank J. "James Buchanan and the Crises of the Union." **Journal of Southern History, IX,** Nov., 1943, 455-474.

Sioussat, St. G.L. "James Buchanan." **American Secretaries of State, V,** 237-336. New York, 1928.

THE ANTE-BELLUM DECADE

Beale, Howard K. "What Historians Have Said about the Causes of the Civil War." In Social Science Research Council, **Theory and Practice in Historical Study: A Report of the Committee on Historiography,** New York, 1946. A valuable guide to the writers and theories on the causes of the Civil War.

Craven, Avery. **The Growth of Southern Nationalism, 1848-1861.** Baton Rouge, 1953. Treats the sociological, political and emotional aspects of the period, with emphasis on the national scene.

Nevins, Allan. **The Emergence of Lincoln.** 2 vols. New York, 1950. This superb study carries his **Ordeal of the Union** through the Buchanan administration. It is undoubtedly the most important historical work for gaining an understanding of the political background of the period.

————. **Ordeal of the Union.** 2 vols. New York, 1947. Covers the period through the Pierce administration up to Buchanan. Invaluable for background.

Nichols, Roy F. **The Disruption of American Democracy.** New York, 1948.* Clearly and coldly portrays the chief political actors, led by Buchanan himself, during the years just before the war. Supported by a mass of documentation and a comprehensive bibliography, this study gives a competent understanding of the workings of politics.

Pressley, Thomas J. **Americans Interpret Their Civil War.** Princeton, 1954.* A scholarly study of historians who have conflicting theories on the causes of the Civil War.

Rozwenc, Edwin C., ed. **Slavery as a Cause of the Civil War.** Boston, 1961.* One of the Amherst **Problems in American Civilization** series. In addition to selections from various historians, it contains excerpts from Buchanan's 1866 book, blaming war on Republican fanaticism.

Smith, Elbert B. **The Death of Slavery, 1837-65.** Chicago, 1967. Excellent brief treatment in one of **The Chicago History of American Civilization** series.

Villard, O.G. **John Brown.** New York, 1943. Less critical than Nevins.

THE PRESIDENCY

Bailey, Thomas A. **Presidential Greatness: The Image and the Man from George Washington to the Present.** New York, 1966.* A critical and subjective study of the qualities of presidential greatness, arranged topically rather than chronologically. The book includes an excellent up to date bibliography on presidential powers and problems, with special emphasis on measuring effectiveness or greatness according to the Bailey criteria.

Binkley, Wilfred E. **The Man in the White House: His Powers and Duties.** Revised ed. New York, 1964.* Treats the development of the various roles of the American president.

Brown, Stuart Gerry. **The American Presidency: Leadership, Partisanship, and Popularity.** New York, 1966. Seems to like the more partisan presidents like Jefferson and Jackson.

Corwin, Edward S. **The President: Office and Powers.** 4th ed. New York, 1957.* An older classic.

Kane, Joseph Nathan. **Facts About the Presidents.** New York, 1959. Includes comparative as well as biographical data about the presidents.

Koenig, Louis W. **The Chief Executive.** New York, 1964. Authoritative study of presidential powers.

Laski, Harold J. **The American Presidency.** New York, 1940.* A classic.

Rossiter, Clinton. **The American Presidency.** 2nd ed. New York, 1960.* Useful.

Schlesinger, Arthur Meier. "Historians Rate United States Presidents," **Life,** XXV (November 1, 1948), 65 ff.

--------. "Our Presidents: A Rating by Seventy-five Historians," **New York Times Magazine,** July 29, 1962, 12 ff.

NAME INDEX

Adams, John Quincy, 4
Anderson, Major Robert, 16, 17
Appleton, John, 19
Ashburton, Lord, 7
Black, Jeremiah S., 11, 16
Breckinridge, John C., 10, 15
Brown, Aaron, 11, 14
Brown, John, 14
Buchanan, Elizabeth Speer, mother,
  1, 5
Buchanan, James, father, 1, 3
Calhoun, John C., 3
Cass, Lewis, 8, 11, 16
Clay, Henry, 4, 5
Clifford, Nathan, 13
Cobb, Howell, 11, 16
Coleman, Ann, 2
Coleman, Robert, 2
Crawford, William H., 4, 5
Crittenden, John J., 13, 16
Curtis, Benjamin Robert, 13
Douglas, Stephen A., 10, 14, 15
English, William H., 13
Fillmore, Millard, 10
Floyd, John B., 11, 17
Fremont, John C., 10
Geary, John W., 11
Grier, Robert C., 11
Hamlin, Hannibal, 15

Harris, Townsend, 13
Harrison, William Henry, 7
Holt, Joseph, 14, 17
Hopkins, James, 1
Jackson, Andrew, 4, 5
Johnson, Herschel V., 15
Lane, Harriet, 9
Lane, Joseph, 15
Lincoln, Abraham, 13, 14, 15, 16, 18
Mason, John Y., 10
Nicholas, I., 5
Pierce, Franklin, 9, 10
Polk, James K., 7
Scott, Dred, 11
Slidell, John, 8
Soule, Pierre, 10
Stanton, Edwin M., 16
Taney, Roger, 11
Thomas, Philip F., 16
Thompson, Jacob, 11, 17
Toucey, Isaac, 11
Trist, Nicholas P., 8
Tyler, John, 7
Van Buren, Martin, 6, 7
Victoria, Queen, 9, 14
Walker, Robert J., 11, 12
Walker, William, 12
Webster, Daniel, 7
Young, Brigham, 12

TITLES IN THE OCEANA
PRESIDENTIAL CHRONOLOGY SERIES

Senior Editor: Howard F. Bremer

Reference books containing Chronology - Documents - Bibliographical Aids for each President covered.

1. GEORGE WASHINGTON   96 pages/$3.00
    edited by Howard F. Bremer

2. JOHN ADAMS   96 pages/$3.00
    edited by Howard F. Bremer

3. JAMES BUCHANAN   96 pages/$3.00
    edited by Irving J. Sloan

4. GROVER CLEVELAND   128 pages/$4.00
    edited by Robert I. Vexler

5. FRANKLIN PIERCE   96 pages/$3.00
    edited by Irving J. Sloan

6. ULYSSES S. GRANT   128 pages/$4.00
    edited by Philip Moran

Books may be ordered from
OCEANA PUBLICATIONS, INC.
Dobbs Ferry, New York 10522